My Bristol
The History and The Culture

Teresa Purkis

ISBN: 1518716369
ISBN-13: 978-1518716362

Contents

My Bristol

1 Introduction.

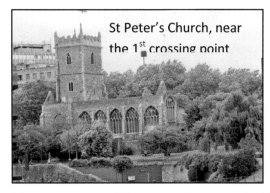
St Peter's Church, near the 1st crossing point

Bristol is the largest city in the south west of England, providing the perfect base to explore the region, with a population of approximately half a million. The city lies between Somerset and Gloucestershire, and is a county in its own right and so is called the City and County of Bristol. Bristol grew up in Saxon times at the confluence of the rivers Avon and Frome. The settlement was known as Brycgstow, the place of the bridge.

The geology of the area has made Bristol what it is today and has given us features such as the Avon Gorge, the Cotswold escarpment, and gentle rolling scenery. It influenced settlements on the banks of the river Avon, and some of the first coal mining in the world. This geology consists of coal, sandstone, mudstone and limestone which offers a rich and varied environment for wildlife and unique species of flora. Some of the rocks are Triassic and Jurassic, and there are Pennant Sandstones of the Carboniferous age.

Avon Gorge

Council House

Bristol is a large cosmopolitan, diverse city; bustling with arts, culture, music, adventure, sports and festivals. It is home to the 2006 UK Museum of the Year, the SS Great Britain, the international balloon fiesta, and is Green Capital 2015. Bristol boasts attractions to suit all tastes and is home to Head Offices in insurance and banking, and the Ministry of Defence. The motto of the city is "Virtute et industria." valour and industry.

Bristol is the main centre of culture, employment and education in the region. It is easy to explore the city either by foot, bus, water or air. There are plenty of walking tours of the city centre, including the pirate trail and the heritage trail. Also there are different companies that run ferry and boat tours of the harbour. Discover more of the city with a sightseeing open top bus or hot air balloon.

Bristol Docks

2 Early Settlements.

Bristol Observatory

Archaeological finds confirm that the first settlers in the Bristol area were in the Palaeolithic era. Five Iron Age hill forts have been found. Two forts were on the Leigh Woods side of the Avon Gorge and two on Kings Weston Hill. Another was on Clifton Down near the Observatory. The Blaise Castle Hill fort and Kings Weston Camp were built first. The hillforts are legally protected as Scheduled Ancient Monuments.

The Romans too settled in the area, building a port in the current Sea Mills known as Portus Abonae, or Abona, complete with wharves to serve the boats that plied their trade in the area. Portus Abonae survives below ground today. It is scheduled under the Ancient Monuments and Archaeological Areas Act. Evidence shows that the Romans settled from the first Century to the later fourth Century. Abona was established as a military town.

Sea Mills

Site of scheduled monument

The early settlement was located to the left of the River Trym on a sloping and terraced bank. Large quantities of pottery and wares were found during various excavations including a cobbled street. Sea Mills was connected by a Roman road to Bath, it crossed the Downs near Stoke Road, and a short length is visible as a slightly raised grassy bank. This is also a scheduled monument.

The roads likely route from Sea Mills was Roman Way, Mariners Drive, Pitch and Pay lane, Julian Road, across the downs and continued onwards towards Bath. 'Via Julia' can be seen on a building in Lower Redland Road (see picture). Another road connected Sea Mills to Gloucester following what is now Cribbs Causeway. The settlement at Sea Mills was likely abandoned in the early 5th century as no evidence of occupation has been found after this time.

Other villas and settlements can be found. These Roman settlements were called Oser nante Badon or places in the valley of Bath, and some were discovered during excavations on Upper Maudlin Street and Lewins Mead in the 1970s. Farm dwellings have been found at Knowle West, Lawrence Weston, Bedminster and Avonmouth, and villas at Kings Weston (pictured) and Brislington, and a village is known to be at Inns Court which was first discovered in 1982. Ruins of a small Villa can be seen from the Portway.

3 Saxon and Medieval Bristol.

The town of Brycgstow, the place of the bridge, was founded around Saxon times, about 450 AD. Anglo-Saxon Brycgstow lay on the north bank of the river Avon, in Mercian territory. A slight ridge of high ground ran between the two rivers, rising clear of the riverside marshes and formed the ideal site on which to build. It was likely a fortified wooden settlement, surrounded by an earthen rampart with a wooden palisade on top.

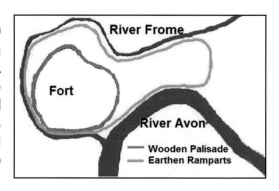

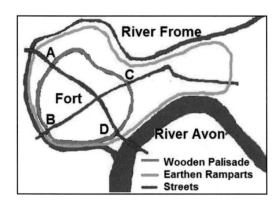

The earliest bridge was further east than today. Bristol became a frontier town against the Britons of South Wales. The four main streets were Broad Street, Corn Street, Winch Street and High Street. The gates into the town were at the end of these streets. The roads led to A Aust, B Sea Mills, C Winchcombe and D Bath. Winch Street became Wine Street of today. Over the next centuries, the name changed from Brycgstow to Bristol due to the local dialect.

In about 930AD a second wall was built closer to the River Frome and the original wall was enlarged to take in St Mary-le-Port and St Peters. New gates were needed and Frome Gate, Giles Gate, Aylwards Gate and Pithay Gate were built. The population in 1066 was about 4,000. In 1088 the wooden fort was replaced by a stone castle further east of St Peters guarding the entrance to the town. It was built originally as a Norman motte and bailey castle. In 1135 it was extended and a great five-storey Keep was built of Caen stone from nearby Brandon Hill. The Castle was built to protect the eastern end of the town.

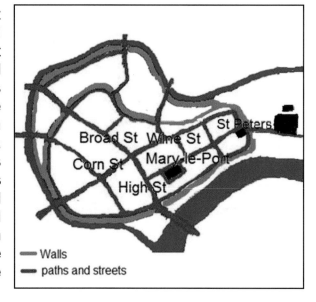

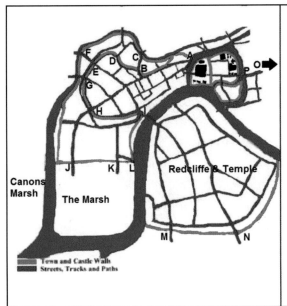

A Newgate
B Aylwards Gate
C Pithay Gate
D St John's Arch
E St John's Gate
F Frome Gate
G St Gile's Gate
H St Leonard's Gate
I St Nicholas' Gate
J Marsh Street Gate
K Back Gate
L Marsh Gate
M Redcliffe Gate
N Temple Gate
O Lawford's Gate
P Nether Gate

The River Frome was diverted and the marshland reclaimed. A moat and ditch was added and the walls were extended around the moat and into the Marsh. Piercing the walls at intervals were fortified gateways. The original seven gates expanded to fourteen. Today some gates are acknowledged by their street names, St John's Arch is still in existence. Redcliffe, at that time, was a separate town, enclosed within its own walls.

Old Market was the entrance to the city from the east and ran to the boundaries of the old castle. Lawford's Gate was built around 1373 when Edward III made Bristol a county corporate as it was important enough to be independent; it included Redcliffe and the Temple area. Their wall became part of Bristol's city wall, very little now remains of the pre-war Temple streets and buildings. South of the river were Redcliffe and Temple Fee. The marshland was given in 1145 to the Knights Templar. These soldier-monks were traders with their own fleet of ships.

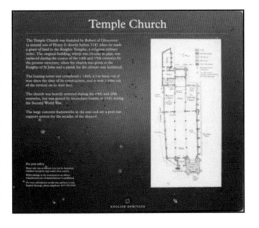

The Saxon bridge was probably timber-built. In the 1240s Bristol replaced it in stone. Bristol Bridge was quickly lined with shops. It became one of the busiest commercial centres of the city. The Chapel of St Mary was above the gate on Bristol Bridge and was finished in 1361. It was closed at the Reformation. In 1768 a new bridge was opened. The centre span is an elliptical 55 feet and the sides are 45 feet semi-circle. Four little shops took tolls. The Georgian bridge is still there, but hidden beneath the broader roadway that was added in Victorian times.

Bristol Bridge today

The town in the Middle Ages was one of the four most prosperous in England. Only small sections of the medieval town wall today exists, by St John's Arch (pictured) and other pieces are hidden away in Castle Park. The heart of the modern city still adheres to this street plan. As prosperity increased, so the city spread outwards. After the Reformation, monastic lands were sold off leading to expansion into the surrounding area.

In 1314 there were eight bridges over the Rivers; Bristol Bridge from High Street to Redcliffe, St Giles Bridge at the bottom of Small Street, Frome Bridge at the bottom of Christmas Street, Monken (Bridewell) Bridge going to St James Priory, Aylward Bridge at the bottom of the Pithay, Merchant Street Bridge leading north from the castle, Elle Bridge at the end of Broadweir and Castle Bridge leading to Old Market.

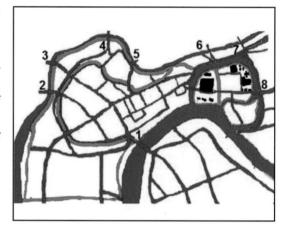

The first Siege of Bristol in 1326 happened during the Despenser wars of September and November. Isabella of France, wife of Edward II, and the 1st Earl of March besieged Bristol for 8 days. The castle was captured after several attacks by battering ram on the gates, and the daughters of Isabella were rescued. Despenser surrendered and was hanged. When finally the war ended Edward II had been murdered in Berkeley Castle and Isabella was regent for Edward III.

4 After the Tudors.

Bristol was a smelly place. The streets had open gutters running down the centre. Storms would wash the mud and dung into the drain and eventually out into the river. The city scavenger or raker would cart off what wasn't washed away and was paid by householders until 1543. Bristol slowly cleaned up and by 1480 there were several public latrines in Bristol. Archaeologists have found stone-lined drains everywhere in central Bristol. Drinking water came from wells. Water was piped from springs on nearby hills to public conduits about the city. St John's Conduit (pictured) is beside St John's Church and until recently still flowed. "Walking the pipe" is a walk from Knowle to St Mary Redcliffe and follows the route of a pipe first constructed in 1190. This walk was made to check that the water in the pipe was still flowing.

Bristol's position on the rivers Frome and Avon, which flow into the Severn, made it an ideal situation for a port. The original quayside was on the tidal river Avon near the present Castle Park, where the bank was steep and the bed of the river stony. The earliest boats to use were suitable for hugging the coast and sailing up rivers for trading with nearby Wales and Ireland. The tight encirclement of Bristol's rivers made good strategic defence but by the 13th Century, the quayside area was too small, so plans were put into place to create more quayside.

Castle Park

The Great Ditch today

There had been a great expansion in trade, bringing cargoes of wine and fine leather from France and Spain. A new harbour was developed by diverting the course of the river Frome. The Great Ditch was excavated through the marshlands belonging to the Abbey of St Augustine and was nearly half a mile long, about 40 yards wide and 18 feet deep. It was completed around 1248 and it cost £5,000 to build (a huge fortune in those days).

Site of old bridgehead

The ditch became St Augustine's Reach and takes its name from the old Abbey, now Bristol Cathedral. Up to the 1960s, cargo ships tied up on this stretch of water and the port was very much part of city life. It was covered over as it flowed through the modern city centre. Evidence of the port is the Church St Mary on the Quay. The bridgehead has now been replaced by the cascade as part of the Millennium changes made to the Centre.

In 1607 Bristol was recovering from the worst floods which killed 501, a possible tsunami. The river Severn had frozen over and navigation was brought to a standstill. The 10,000 residents of Bristol faced a disastrous harvest. The citizens had seized on November 5th as party night, so two years after the Gunpowder Plot the Corporation decreed a civic celebration and Bonfire Night. Soon every town and village had its own bonfire night party.

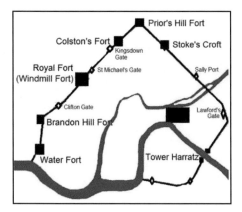

During the English Civil War Bristol's status as the second city, after London, made control of its wealth and port one of the chief objectives of both Parliament and the King. In 1642 a new outer wall of earthworks were started to strengthen against siege warfare. The wall started at Water Fort which appears to be near Jacobs Wells Road/Hotwells Road, north to Brandon Hill, then North East to Prior's Hill Fort, (Kingsdown Parade/ Freemantle Road), South East to Lawfords Gate, finally onward to Tower Harratz and the old Redcliffe walls.

During the Civil War Bristol changed hands a couple of times. Prince Rupert seized it from the Parliament in 1643. Some of the earthworks were realigned and heightened. Windmill Hill Fort was replaced by a large pentagonal fort and was used as Rupert's Headquarters, he renamed it the Great Fort or Royal Fort. The work was still being completed in 1645 when the parliamentarians began their assault on the city.

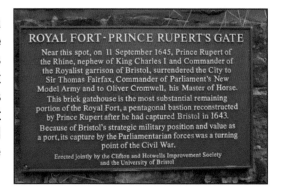

Rupert lost the city to Sir Thomas Fairfax. Wickham Court, Stapleton (pictured) is a historic Grade II-listed house. General Sir Thomas Fairfax met there with Oliver Cromwell in 1645 for a cabinet of war meeting before the attack by the New Model Army on Bristol Castle. There were days of fighting which ended months of hunger and hardship for the citizens of Bristol and one of the Civil War's longest sieges. 200 royalist soldiers lost their lives. There is a blue plaque to commemorate this meeting.

Parliamentarians attacked the lines between Prior's Hill Fort and Colston's Fort. In 1655, Cromwell made the citizens of Bristol meet the cost of destroying the works. Of the Royal Fort, only the gate house remains. The Castle had by Tudor times faded in significance. For 600 years the castle was the most visible building in Bristol, but Cromwell ordered the destruction of it in 1656 to make armed insurrection more difficult.

The 18th Century brought more settled times and large building works began, including Queens Square (pictured). Narrow roadways were widened, new thoroughfares were constructed. Old properties were demolished and replaced by banks, company headquarters, offices and other commercial premises. By the turn of the century Bristol gained something of a radical reputation and in 1793 eleven died during rioting provoked by an increased bridge toll. Furthermore, in 1831 major riots broke out when a reform bill was blocked.

In 1888 Bristol was made a county borough and the office of Lord Mayor was established. Bristol was forced to give up its county status in 1974 as part of a government reshuffling of county boundaries. The new County of Avon was divided into six districts Bath, Kingswood, Northavon, Wansdyke, Woodspring and Bristol. In 1996 the County of Avon was abolished and the area was divided into BANES (Bath and North-East Somerset), North Somerset, South Gloucester and the City and County of Bristol. In 2015 Bristol is England's sixth most populous city and is a member of the Core Cities Group.

On 24 November 1940, 5,000 incendiary and 10,000 high explosive bombs were dropped on the city. The attack started at 6.30pm with some 12,000 incendiary bombs and 160 tons of high-explosive bombs dropping. Within an hour 70 fires had started. 207 people were killed and thousands of houses, businesses and 35 churches destroyed or damaged including Temple Church (pictured). The City Centre, Park Street and surrounds, including the area that is now Castle Park, which had been the main shopping area, were badly damaged. On 3 – 4 January 1941 Bristol had its longest raid lasting 12 hours. The last raid on Bristol was on 15 May 1944.

5 Early Trade.

There have been more than three hundred separate industries during the history of Bristol. From the 12th Century Woad from Picardy was imported as a source of blue dye and trade continued to flourish throughout the following century. It not only provided blue dye, but was also used in the mixing of other colours. Woad was eventually replaced by the stronger indigo and then by synthetic indigoes.

A scarlet dye came from Portugal. The dye is taken from the dried bodies of a scale insect that lived in the Kermes oak tree. The word crimson is derived from kermes due to the widespread use of this dye and the rich red colour that it yields. In Bristol, woollen cloth from Somerset and Gloucestershire was woven, cotton and leather were manufactured then all were dyed. These were the main exports from the port.

Bristol expanded across the Avon into Redcliffe and Temple. This area became a centre for wool merchants, weavers, fullers and dyers. The term 'adventurers' was given to those who traded overseas in cloth and other goods. From this group of merchants evolved the Society of Merchant Venturers, who controlled the port of Bristol for centuries. The round church of the Templars was replaced at the end of the 14th Century to include a Weavers' Chapel (pictured).

By the 13th century wine was the main import and by the Middle Ages it was imported from Spain and Portugal as well as France. There was also a large brewing industry. Cod could only be dried and salted on land, it is likely Bristolian sailors were fishing in the Grand Banks, and salting their catch ashore in North America a decade before Christopher Columbus crossed the Atlantic. Bristolians kept quiet about this New World.

Since the 12th century the wine trade with England's territory in Aquitaine boomed, and this business extended soon to Spanish and Portuguese wineries. At its height about 3000 "tuns" were imported and half of Bristol's wine was brought in Bristol's ships. The wars with France and Spain hit trade, but the Portugal trade route continued. In the 1790's Avery's wine and Harvey's sherry house began. In 1949 Harvey's stopped importing direct into the city, and in 2003 Harvey's departed the city, leaving Avery's as the only long-established wine merchant.

Rope had been made in the city prior to Edward II. The King levied a tax on the import of hemp during his reign. The starting length needed to be one third to a half longer than the length of the finished product. Early maps show there were rope makers at Broadweir, and St Augustine's reach, but it is known rope walks were in Temple and Redcliffe Backs, the Marsh and St Philips Marsh, plus others. Traditional rope-making stopped in the 1960's but the Bristol Rope and Twine Company still makes rope using modern methods and materials.

6 The Rivers, Brooks and Streams.

There are four rivers that flow through modern Bristol; the Avon, Frome, Malago and Trym. The River Avon rises in the northern limit of Wiltshire passing through Melksham, Bradford and Bath. Until 1727 the River Avon was not navigable further than Bristol. It used to be a series of streams broken by swamps and ponds, with serious flooding every winter. Now it is managed by a series of weirs and locks and is navigable to Bath and beyond.

River Avon towards Bath

Through the Avon Gorge

Bristol developed at the point where it was convenient to cross and where ships could be carried up on the tidal current in the river Avon. The twisting river has one of the highest tides, with about 30 feet between high and low tide. The tidal range of the Bristol Channel and River Severn is the second greatest of any in the world, making travel by sea difficult. Bristol was a popular destination for cargo ships and it became impossible to accommodate them all.

At each high tide too many ships were trying to reach or leave the Bristol port. Ships were sometimes stranded in the river on the way to Bristol, causing damage to them and delays to others. On monthly neap tides there was never enough water in the river for the larger ships to move, so they would have to wait for a week or two in Bristol or at the mouth of the Avon until there were suitable sailing conditions, further congesting the port.

Low tide outside the floating harbour

Modern Bristol docks after introduction of the floating harbour

At low tide, all the ships in port went aground and shipping was stranded in the mud for considerable lengths of time, causing extreme stress on the boats. The phrase 'Shipshape and Bristol fashion' was coined to describe a ship that was of high enough quality to withstand the rigours of entering, docking and leaving Bristol's port. The floating harbour negated the effects of the tide so that ships could safely dock.

The Conham Ferry still runs from Beeses Tea Gardens to the Hanham side, and is the oldest river ferry crossing on the River Avon. Beeses was founded in 1846 by Mrs Beese, who discouraged the drinking of alcohol. She provided refreshments to the many travellers using the Conham Ferry, the captain of which was Mr Beese. Today's cream teas are enjoyed in a 1960s building, and the gardens are enjoyed by travellers coming from road or river.

A park lies on the site of a former sewage works which served part of Kingswood until 1968. The views from the Feeder to Conham changed from idyllic countryside, to the noise and pollution of heavy industry, then transformed again, with tree-planting, extensive new housing and pleasant river walks. Troopers Hill is a nature reserve full of history, wild plants and animals. The chimneys on Troopers Hill remain.

Crews Hole Development from the River Avon

Navigation Station near the Horseshoe Bend

Towards Avonmouth is Horseshoe Bend, an 11 acre biological Site of Special Scientific Interest, consisting of a wooded cliff and a narrow salt marsh. Navigation lights help ships through this section. Nearby are the remains of the Powder House, built in the 1770's. Ships were forced to offload any gunpowder and inflammable substances before proceeding to the port to reduce the danger of fire. The previous gunpowder store was by Temple Meads. The Powder House is now a residential building.

Modern yachts and boat use the moorings on Ham Green Lakes and Pill Creek. Pill Creek is where the first emigrant Methodists started their journey to America. On the south bank the Pill Hobblers were based, and were responsible for transferring cargoes onto smaller vessels and hauling or towing these into the city docks. Today tugs are used and the hobblers are responsible for mooring of all vessels at Portbury, Avonmouth and the City Docks.

Pill Creek

1976 saw the final large ship launched in the docks. Avonmouth is 8 miles downstream from the city centre. In 1865 the deep water Royal Edward Dock was constructed at Avonmouth. Portbury dock is the latest addition, and was specially constructed to deal with tankers and container vessels. In 2013 Avonmouth welcomed the cruise ship MV Discovery, as the departure point for her summer itinerary. In 2014 Fred Olson also used the port, but due to the size of the locks only the smaller ships can dock.

Avonmouth Docks

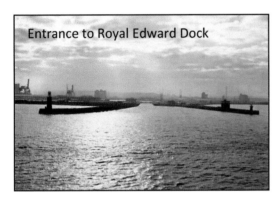

Entrance to Royal Edward Dock

During WWI, Shirehampton had a remount depot for horses, with a capacity of 5,000 horses. The Royal Edward Dock had 347,045 horses and mules passing through throughout the war. Avonmouth started production of mustard gas, and by the end 85,424 mustard gas shells had been made. In World War II the docks were enlarged adding more facilities and an oil products supply pipeline to London via the Pipelines and Storage System.

The source of the River Frome rises in Dodington Park in the Cotswold Hills. It flows through Chipping Sodbury, then south of Winterbourne Down, Frenchay, Oldbury Court, Snuff Mills and Eastville Park through to the city centre. Since the 13th Century it helped power early industries. The Frome originally flowed from Stone Bridge (by St John's Gate) along the line of St Stephen's Street and Baldwin Street, joining the Avon near Bristol Bridge.

The Frome at Broom Hill Stapleton

Over the years the Frome has been widened, straightened, deepened and culverted. The river was crossed by a drawbridge roughly where Clare Street meets Broad Quay. Evidence of a port is shown by St Mary on the Quay (pictured) and Quay Street. As ships became bigger the influence of the Frome lessened. Now the river passes through a culvert which runs under the Centre. It was covered over in stages, from the 19th century to the late 1930s.

Bell Hill, Stapleton

There were 13 bridges over the river in the city centre area. Most of the single arch stone bridges were destroyed as the Frome was gradually culverted. More were lost with the building of the M32, dividing communities in two, leaving only the road bridges at Bell Hill Stapleton, Muller Road, New Stadium Road in Eastville and Junction3 of the M32. Other road bridges within the A4174 ring road are Broom Hill, Stapleton and Cleevewood, Frenchay.

Under Cleevewood bridge is an earlier arch, possibly medieval. In the 18th Century there was a tollgate for the upkeep of the roads. A post marked 'Turnpike Trust 1823' can still be seen today. On the 2 mile stretch of river Frome valley between the road bridges of Cleevewood and Broom Hill are Frenchay and Halfpenny bridges. Frenchay Bridge (pictured) is a single span arch bridge. It has a cast iron plaque which reads "Frenchay Bridge, built by subscription". It is closed to motor vehicles.

Halfpenny Bridge is and always was a footbridge. It crosses the river from Snuff Mills Park to Oldbury Court Park. The original stone pillars remain but it has new spans. Between Eastville and Stapleton is Wickham Bridge. Wickham Bridge (pictured) is said to be the oldest bridge in Bristol. The medieval bridge was washed away in the floods of 1968 and was on the old road to Gloucester. It was rebuilt and is now only for pedestrians, motorcyclists and cyclists.

The Malago source is on Dundry Hill and is culverted through much of Bristol before emerging through storm drains into the New Cut opposite the entrance to the Bathurst Basin. Until the 19th century, the Malago flowed into the Avon at Treen Mills, Redcliffe. The River Trym is a short river which rises in Filton. The upper reaches are through culverts and emerges through a nature reserve and a park before joining the River Avon at Sea Mills.

The Malago in Bedminster

Remains of harbour walls

The harbour of the Trym at Sea Mills was built in 1712, when it was one of three in Britain where boats could remain afloat regardless of the tide. As the cargoes had to be delivered to the city by barge the port failed. In 1750 a whale fishery company was formed. The whales were taken into the dock and the blubber boiled there. The company closed in 1761. You can still see some remains of the harbour walls but the harbour itself is used only for mooring pleasure craft.

In 1803, a 70 acre harbour was created by Jessop. The Avon was dammed in three places to create the 70 acre city docks, allowing ships to permanently float without risk of grounding. It is known as the Floating Harbour. A new river was created, called the New Cut, which stayed tidal and it took five years to complete, using over 1000 English and Irish navvies. Two new road bridges were built at Redcliffe road and Bath road. It is never more than one kilometre south of the harbour. The harbour is fed by the Feeder Canal

Feeder Canal

Floating harbor taken from Redcliffe Bridge

The Floating Harbour follows the original route of the Avon and meanders through Bristol city centre. The harbour re-joins the tidal river (New Cut) at the Cumberland Basin. The second weir, the Overfall Dam, controlled the water level at the outward end of the Harbour. The non-tidal parts vary in depth from about a metre to over four metres. The Harbour grew as a busy commercial port until it closed in 1975.

The Cumberland Basin was built with two entrance locks from the tidal Avon and a junction lock between the Basin and the Floating Harbour. The Basin was used as a lock when there were large numbers of arrivals and sailings. The Feeder Canal between Temple Meads and Netham provides the link to the tidal river so that boats could continue upstream to Bath.

Netham Locks

The Bathhurst and Totterdown locks allowed small craft to enter The New Cut at either end. The Bathhurst lock (pictured) was blocked during WW2 as a precaution and was never reopened. Weirs and locks control the level of the Harbour water and allow excess to spill back into the tidal river Avon. The lock gates ensure that extreme high spring tides that come over Netham weir do not enter the city and are part of the City Docks Capital Project upgrade.

In the 1850s a network of foul water channels were dug in Bristol to carry excess into the Floating Harbour. The River Frome discharges into the Floating Harbour at 4 locations Castle Ditch, Fosseway, Castle Green Tunnel, which runs under Castle Park, and the Frome Culvert. During intense rainfall the Victorian sewers still couldn't cope which resulted in areas being swamped with water. A seven-mile long sewer was built to the Avon helping prevent flooding.

The Victorians warned that the city's sewerage infrastructure needed significant investment and a plan was devised to modernise it, but to no avail. Until the 1960s about 40 million gallons of untreated sewage was discharged into the Avon daily. The stench made some areas unbearable and affected the local environment. To reduce the smell chlorine was poured into the river with further consequences for aquatic life. Sewage treatment works at Avonmouth (pictured) were constructed between 1960 and 1964.

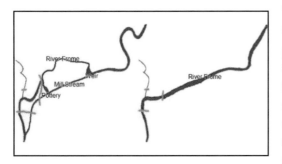

The mill dams at Baptist Mills prevented the free flow and flooding that happened regularly. The pottery closed there in 1891. The Corporation demolished the pottery and the mill to try to stop the continual flooding. It straightened, widened and deepened the course of the Frome. The culverting can still be seen where the river is exposed between Baptist Mills and River Street, and under the M32, but this did not fully alleviate the problem.

In the 1960s the first of four large construction projects began, but it wasn't soon enough for the great flood of 1968. 13cm of rain fell in 24 hours. The low lying areas of the city soon began to flood up to 3m, especially around the Avon, Frome, Malago and Trym valleys. Bedminster, Brislington and Hartcliffe were damaged, and over 300 homes were flooded. Bristol City FC and Eastville Stadium, Bristol Rovers home, had over 5 million gallons of flood water pumped out.

The Northern Stormwater Interceptor, running from the river Frome Eastville Sluices (pictured) to the River Avon by Clifton Suspension Bridge, was constructed to control the River Frome. Six years later, the southern foul sewer started to take sewage to the sewage treatment works. The Malago storm water interceptor was built between 1971 and 1974. Sewerage services in the Bristol area are provided by Wessex Water.

Cumberland Basin under flood water

The Bristol Tunnel in 2009 is linked to the northern foul interceptor. However during extremely high tides the river Avon is susceptible. The Cumberland Basin, City Centre and the Broadmead area still remains at risk of flooding during severe weather conditions. The City Council have a strategic flood plan in place and have purchased storm surge barriers to protect the low lying areas. They can also release water from the floating harbour.

Countless streams flow down from the surrounding hills, Pennywell Springs, Brislington Brook, Pigeonhouse stream, St Anne's Spring, Siston Brook, Cutlers Mill brook, Warmley Brook and Horfield Brook all find their way into the rivers. A ford in Henbury (pictured) is passable on most days of the year where the Hazel (Hen) Brook flows under the road. When heavy rains arrive and the ford floods, the traffic can be diverted over a nearby small bridge.

7 River Avon Industries.

Crew's Hole is just over two miles up-river of Bristol Bridge. It is east of Bristol, the traditional side of a city for smelly works because of the prevailing winds. There were stone for quarrying, coal from both open-cast mining and pits nearby in Conham and Hanham, and clay suitable for a fireclay works. It was an industrial area from the 18th century when copper smelting was started by the Bristol Brass Company.

Many works grew up along the River Avon including the Tar works, Netham Chemical Works, the Sheldon Bush Lead Works, Avon Board Mills, a pottery, barge building and a bottle-glass works. The River Avon provided the means for moving the materials. The companies employed small fleets to deliver goods either to the railway yards, the canal barges, coasting vessels or ships bound for foreign ports, which were in the docks. Return cargoes were the raw materials needed.

Netham Bridge

The Clarks Wood Company started importing hardwoods in 1798. It is now part of the Premier Forest Group. The warehouse in Silverthorn Lane is a 19th-century industrial building. It dates from about 1863, but only two of its original walls remain. It is known to have been used early in its history as a railhead warehouse. It is an example of the Bristol Byzantine style of architecture, and has been listed by English Heritage as a grade II listed building.

In the 18th century, copper ore was brought by boat, mainly from Cornwall and north Devon and coal was sourced locally. From about 1750 the Brass Company started casting the waste copper slag into moulds to produce black building blocks. The Black Castle was built using these blocks for William Reeve in the 1760's. Reeve was made bankrupt in 1774. Arno's Vale and the Black Castle were sold. The Black Castle is now a pub.

Making brass items, also supplied a large part of the goods to trade for enslaved Africans. The demand for brassware from the slave trade boosted the industry and kept many men in employment. The industry was for a long time of greater economic significance than the lead-shot industry. Zinc was abundant in the Mendips, and, with local coal and Cornish copper readily available, Bristol was a natural centre for brass-making. In around 1780 the Bristol Brass and Wire Company moved its copper smelting operations to Warmley and by about 1790 the Crews Hole site was abandoned.

William Champion patented a zinc distillation process in 1738 which allowed large scale zinc production. Zinc ore was sealed in large pots with charcoal and heated in a furnace. The zinc vapour descended through condensing pipes to reach a water-filled vessel. This vapour infused the copper. Unfortunately he became bankrupt in 1769. However, zinc smelting continued until 1880. Calamine Brass is made from two-sevenths fine copper, four-sevenths zinc ore calamine, and one-seventh old brass.

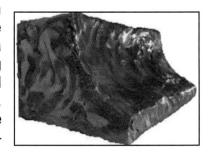

Saltford Brassmill is the only surviving building still with a furnace and working water wheel from the mills making brass and copper goods in the Avon Valley. The mill started in the 1720s and ceased working in 1924. Battery mills were large water-powered hammers that beat the brass ingots into sheet, and then faster hammers shaped the sheet into hollow-ware. The rolling mill produced brass sheets more evenly than hammers. It is a scheduled Ancient Monument and most important remains of the brass industry in England.

The Netham Alkali works in the 1840s, produced sulphuric acid, washing soda and super-phosphates. The company was taken over by I.C.I. and this factory closed after the WW2, opening at Severnside for the production of ethylene oxide, glycol, ammonia and fertilisers. The Naphtha Refinery shut down in the 1960s. The tar distillation plant at Crew's Hole was one of the most modern in Europe following modifications under BSC ownership between 1970 and 1981 but economics led to its closure.

Site of Alkali works

John Bethell, born in Bristol in 1804, made creosote oil to preserve timber. Isambard Kingdom Brunel needed a good preservative for his wooden sleepers and with the technical expertise of Bethell, set up a Tar Works at Crew's Hole in 1843 making creosote and pitch. By 1863 Brunel's manager, William Butler, became owner; he also owned Saltford Brassmill. The Crew's Hole sites were cleared by 1982 and there are now housing estates on both sides of the river.

With the invention of the internal combustion engine the tar industry started separating motor benzole. The Crew's Hole works was at the forefront of this development in 1890. In 1903 a subsidiary was formed called The British Refined Motor Spirit Co. When the 1904 Motor Act came into force, Butlers' registered the first motorcar in Bristol. Its number was AE 1.

Before 1838 cotton was produced in the city on a small scale. Later, the Great Western Cotton Works by the Feeder Canal rivalled any in the country in size. The Cotton Mill on Great Western Lane was designed by Isambard Kingdom Brunel. The factory had its own bleaching works, foundry and engineering establishment. There were workshops to spin and weave cotton. The sheds contained up to 1600 looms. In 1839 there were 958 employees of which were 113 boys, 117 men, 609 were girls and 119 women. The factory closed in 1925.

The factory used pauper children from the workhouse to work for low pay and long hours, and was responsible for the working-class districts around Barton Hill. The American Civil War (1861-1865) and the effect it had on the import of cotton led to a period of closure. This had a catastrophic effect on the families who worked in the factory and many local children died. In 1889 the Barton Hill Cotton Worker's Strike fighting poverty lasted a month. The mill survived for nearly a century. The main spinning mill was demolished in 1968 and now all that remains are the street names.

St Anne's Board Mill Co Ltd was located on the south bank of the river Avon. The mill was established in 1912 and by the early 1930's it was running four machines. The Board Mill was a principal supplier of carton and other board for packing. The coating mill treated the board with a special surface for high quality colour printing. In wartime container board incorporated pitch which remained watertight in tropical conditions.

By 1958 most of the packaging was tied up with the tobacco industry. In 1966 the mills won a Queen's Award for Industry. New markets were found in cereals, pharmaceuticals and chocolate. The annual output in the 1970's reached 160,000 tons. In 1984, with losses running at £200,000 a week, the company that was once one of the country's top three board makers shut up shop. All that remains is the social club situated in Avonvale Road

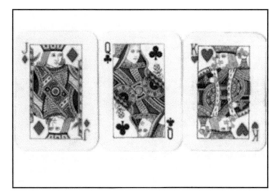

Mardon's, once a giant of the printing and packaging industry, started out in 1823 when a small printing and engraving business was established producing headed notepaper and address cards. In 1849 they started mass-producing labels. They began printing the packets and cards for Will's, then Bristol's biggest tobacco producers. When complete, these miniature packs of cards could be exchanged for full-sized packs. In 1902 they became part of the Imperial Tobacco group. In WW2 it lost 10 of the 13 factories. Lawson Mardon Packaging is still in operation.

8 River Frome Industries.

The Frome at Stapleton

Mills and their associated trades were the main industries on the River Frome. Near the mouth of the river were two mills. Castle Mill was where Broadweir and Merchant Street met, and where Broadweir gets its name. It is likely to be the grist mill which served the castle. Baldwin's Cross Mill was at the bottom of St Nicholas steps, close to the old town, where the River Frome originally flowed into the Avon.

Abraham Darby started making brass at Baptist Mills in 1702. It was originally a grist mill. It was the first commercially successful brass works in Britain. Baptist Mills is viewed by some as the birthplace of the industrial revolution. Darby then established the Cheese Lane Foundry in 1704. Initially he cast brass pots, but by 1705, he moved on to using iron. All Darby's brass making was later transferred to Keynsham's Avon Mill around 1706, because the River Avon had a better water supply and transport links than the River Frome.

Keynsham Brass Mill

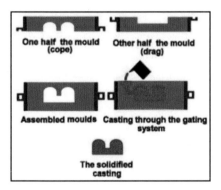
One half the mould (cope)   Other half the mould (drag)

Assembled moulds   Casting through the gating system

The solidified casting

The Brassmill played an integral part in the development of the brass manufacturing industry in Britain by adapting Dutch techniques. Darby developed a method for casting pots in 'greensand' moulds, previously only used for smaller castings. This enabled pots to be mass-produced. The brass was made from ores refined at Crew's Hole and mixed with calamine to make calamine brass. By the 1850s zinc metal was used instead of calamine.

The final brass battery pans ever made in Britain were produced at the Brassmill in June 1927. Now a pub-restaurant, the name has stayed the same as an acknowledgement of its heritage. It still overlooks the river, the mill pond and weir. There is access to the Kennet & Avon Canal. Saltford Brass Mill dates from the 1720s is listed as Grade II* and is also a Scheduled Ancient Monument.

Keynsham Brass mill

In 1839 the former Harford Brass Battery Company at Baptist Mills, which closed in 1814, became a pottery. The business was known as J and J White Pottery. It included a melting house, a charcoal house, a dwelling house, yards and a chapel. Their products were Egyptian black and Rockingham teapots, gold lustre ware, tobacco pipes and a Stone-ware Glaze which was leadless and resistant to acids. The pottery was handed down through the family and by 1861 it was called the Phoenix pottery. Bristol rivalled any in the country and was second only to London in decorative pottery.

Hassell and Cogan tannery used other parts of the mill. Evidence of the structures were destroyed with the building of the M32. The only remains are the street names Millpond Street and Baptist Mills Court, and Millpond School. Bristol was a major centre of the leather industry from medieval times producing some of the best leather in the country. Thomas Ware & Sons in Bedminster is the last, remaining the only full-scale tannery in the UK.

Frome means brisk, the river drops nearly 50 feet between Frenchay and Eastville Park. The water was harnessed and powered eight mills. The mills were all undershot mills meaning they did not need mill ponds. This is the oldest type of water wheel and the least effective. They were grist mills. In the 18th century taking snuff became popular and mills changed production to help serve the local tobacco industries.

In the 1600's the river valley was pitted with quarrying the local Pennant stone, and in the surrounding forests open cast mines were dug for coal. Old quarry workings can be found around Snuff Mills Park. These quarries are now disused, have been filled in and become overgrown. The Pennant Sandstone could easily be cut into blocks for construction works and many of the buildings, cottages, walls and bridges around the Frome Valley are made of it.

Building made of Pennant sandstone

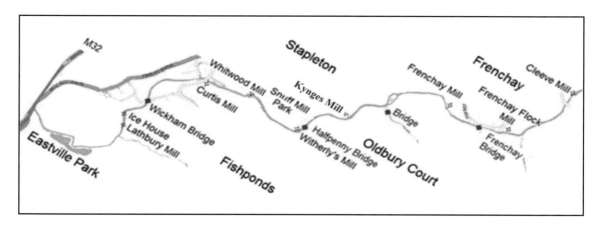

Of the eight mills only Cleeve Mill survives today as a private residence, and the restored Snuff Mill (pictured) can also be found. It contains a waterwheel and an 1850 egg-ended boiler which provided power for a 12hp steam engine. It is the only one in its original setting, and it is the remains of a vertical steam engine. After 1889 the engine was used for powering a six-bladed saw, cutting and crushing stone from the many quarries.

The weirs along the river show where the mills used to be. Lathbury Grist mill is the first mill upstream of Eastville Park, nearby is the remains of an ice house. The next weir is where Broom Hill Bridge crosses the Frome (site pictured). Curtis grist mill was situated here but all evidence disappeared when the road was widened. On the 1880 map it is named as Frome Mill, by the 1890 map it had vanished. The next mill has been known by different names, Whitwood, Stapleton and Snuff Mill.

Snuff Mills Park was purchased in 1926 by the Corporation. The building nearest the river was three stories high but the two upper floors were removed for safety reasons. It has been used as a bandstand. Six buildings, the mill house, stable, piggeries, wagon house and sheds', were also demolished. The ranger's house was built in 1936. The building and the iron waterwheel have been refurbished and restored by the Fishponds Local History Society between 1979 and 1993 (pictured).

By Halfpenny Bridge (pictured) was Witherley's Mill, also called Lower Snuff Mill. It was a grist mill from about 1498, but in 1790 snuff was ground there. In 1792 it became a W. D. & H.O. Wills snuff mill until 1843 then it was used in the manufacturing of flocks and carding wool. It had been abandoned before 1880. Further up the river was Upper Snuff Mill or Kynges Mill. It too started life as a grist mill and from 1771 onwards a snuff mill, until being abandoned before 1880. Frenchay Mill was also a snuff and flour mill.

Frenchay flock mill was the last to be used. It was an iron works until 1880, after which it changed its use to a flock mill and produced mattress fillings. Cleeve mill was originally a grist mill and was converted prior to 1798 to an iron mill. In 1810, these two mills formed the Frenchay Iron Company and had a good reputation both here and abroad. It made giant hoes for use in the plantations in the West Indies.

Other mills grew up on the tributary streams of the River Frome. Cutlersmill brook fed Cutler's Mills and Terrett's mill. Terrett's has had a variety of uses. A Smith's Shop, a dye house, a grist mill and a snuff mill. Finally it was changed into swimming baths, a coffee house, a Bowling Green, teagardens and Inn but closed in 1916. In 1922 it became a builder's yard; today it is the site of Montpelier health centre. The Old England Inn (pictured) is the last remaining of this old group of buildings.

Cutler's Mill is mentioned in 1651, but burned down in 1664. Ashleyvale mill (pictured) and Hooks mill were on Boiling Well Brook on the western side of Ashley Hill. Ashleyvale was first mentioned as 'Glaspelmull' in 1391 and Glass Mill in 1528. It produced ivory black from bone in 1813 and was a flour mill in 1884, but disused by 1898. The pumping station for Quay pipe, which served clean water for the city, is next to the mill. Hooks Mills 1668-1911 was a Flour Mill.

9 The Floating Harbour.

These diagrams show the how the two main rivers have evolved over the centuries.

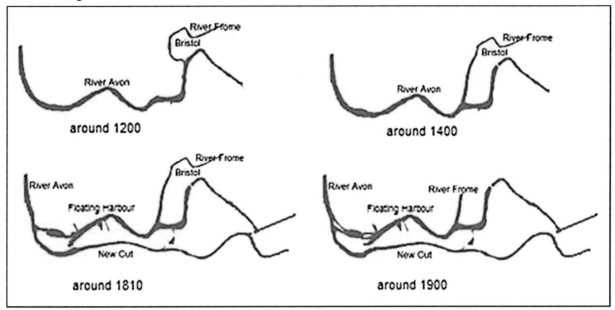

Jessop built Cumberland Basin with two entrance locks and a junction lock. The original junction lock into the Harbour was blocked after the new Junction Lock was built in the late 1860s. The southern entrance lock was 33 feet wide and about 180 feet long. In the 1840s, Brunel modified the lock to make it 52 feet wide and 245 long. The new lock had floating hinged gates and the ballast chambers were prone to silting up because tidal water.

The junction lock houses the stop gates, which are closed when the tide in the river is expected to rise higher than the Harbour level. These tides are known as 'stopgate tides' or 'on a level' These gates are an essential part of Bristol's flood defence system. The wrought-iron swing bridge that formerly crossed Brunel's lock, used the tubular construction that Brunel had used before. The new swing bridge was installed in 1925. Brunel's lock was finally closed in the 1930's.

Jessop's Lock

The overfall dam was a stone structure with a slit to let off flood water. Closing off the harbour trapped sewage and evil-smelling mud in the harbour. In 1832 Brunel was approached and he was asked to design a replacement. It was a series of sluices and locks, known as the Underfall, and a special dredger known as a 'drag boat,' which kept the harbour silt-free. The dragboat, for scraping mud away from the sides of the harbour was eventually scrapped in 1961.

Dredging made use of the four Underfall Sluices. Bottom-opening hopper barges dumped mud into the sluice which was then released into the River Avon. Shallow sluices control the water level and deep sluices remove the silt. When the deep sluices are opened at low tide, a powerful undertow sucks the silt out of the harbour and into the new cut. In 1988, the sluice control was computerised and automated.

Underfall Sluices

Brunel's Lock

Brunel's ships the Great Western and the Great Britain were built in the dry dock. Jessop's northern entrance lock was where the SS Great Britain nearly came to grief as she left Bristol in 1844. The lock was 45 feet wide and 180 feet long. Brunel's 48-foot beam ship was fractionally too big to go through. Coping stones and lock gate platforms had to be removed to allow the ship to finally set sail in 1845. She is not the only structure to suffer this fate.

In 1872, the present entrance lock was opened. It can hold ships 62 feet wide and 350 feet long. Nothing larger can safely navigate the river because of the stretch of river called the horseshoe bend and the tidal range. The Pumphouse housed the original hydraulic pumping system for operating the lock gates and bridges of the 1870s locks. It was superseded by the Underfall Yard system in the late 1880s. A large stretch of the harbour, quay walls and bollards have listed building status.

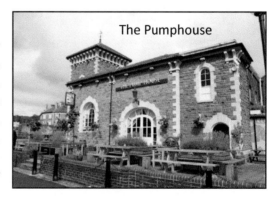
The Pumphouse

The Underfall Yard is named after the sluices that control the level of water in the Harbour. This is where the tidal river Avon was originally dammed by the overfall to create the Floating Harbour in 1809, and remains the operational centre for maintenance and operation of all the lock gates, bridges and leisure activities today. The Docks Engineer installed the facilities in the 1880s and is now a Scheduled Ancient Monument. A Trust fosters traditional boat-building and repair skills.

The original Patent Slipway was built in 1850's and was replaced in the 1890s. Ships were floated onto the cradle and secured. The cradle was then drawn out of the water with a steam-driven winch. The device was a low-cost alternative to dry docks for maintenance and repair work. It was driven by a hydraulic engine powered by the dock's hydraulic system. In 1924, an electric motor was installed which still operates today. It fell into disuse by 1974 but was rebuilt by members of the Slipway Co-operative and Underfall Trust in 1998-99 for long-term preservation as an historic industrial monument.

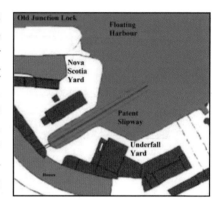

Plimsoll bridge

Cumberland Basin was expensive to build. It was designed as a half-tidal basin, enabling ships to arrive and leave for some hours either side of high tide. The flyover, Plimsoll Bridge, was built in the mid-1960s allowing free movement between opposite sides of the river and uses an electro-hydraulic system using oil at a pressure of 4,480 psi, and opens and closes in three minutes to allow ships to pass.

Although harbour / river water may look brown and dirty, it is full of life and very clean. The brown colour is caused by mud mixed in with the water. However, the harbour hasn't always been so clean as most of Bristol's sewage flowed into the water, polluting it. Nowadays, the water is tested every week to make sure it is safe and clean for people and wildlife. Many different types of fish are found in the harbour. Fishermen commonly catch bream, roach and eels.

The water itself is now home to a multitude of small craft, floating restaurants and leisure activities. Avon Rowing club, sailing and canoeing schools attract youngster and adults alike. Small boats use the water for recreational purposes and larger ones are still able to access and dock up to Narrow Quay. Bristol University and the University of the West of England stage their annual boat races here.

Powerboat racing was staged in the docks proving a very popular and taxing event. However after a few fatalities it was halted. A variety of festivals and regattas provide a colourful addition to proceedings, and the annual Harbour Festival has become a magnet, with up to a quarter of a million people visiting each year. Take a walk using the Brunel Mile and City Docks MP3 Tour, or a self-guided tour of Banksy's most famous Bristol works. The Run Bristol event ranges from 100m to 1 mile.

10 The Wharfs and Docks.

The diagram shows the two rivers, new cut and feeder today, as well as the position of the wharfs, docks, locks, backs and basins.

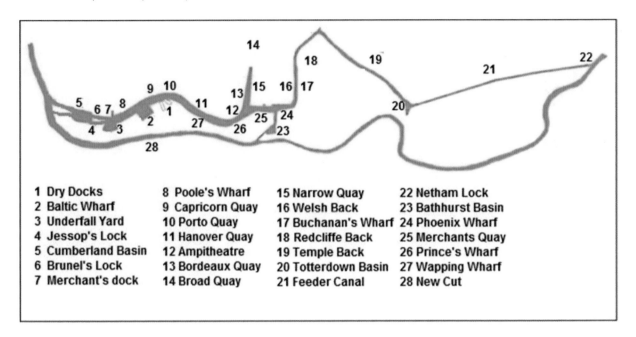

1 Dry Docks	8 Poole's Wharf	15 Narrow Quay	22 Netham Lock
2 Baltic Wharf	9 Capricorn Quay	16 Welsh Back	23 Bathhurst Basin
3 Underfall Yard	10 Porto Quay	17 Buchanan's Wharf	24 Phoenix Wharf
4 Jessop's Lock	11 Hanover Quay	18 Redcliffe Back	25 Merchants Quay
5 Cumberland Basin	12 Ampitheatre	19 Temple Back	26 Prince's Wharf
6 Brunel's Lock	13 Bordeaux Quay	20 Totterdown Basin	27 Wapping Wharf
7 Merchant's dock	14 Broad Quay	21 Feeder Canal	28 New Cut

Prince's Wharf was built up in the 1860s, it had long been a shipbuilding area, and it's here that Brunel built his first ship, the Great Western in 1837. The Great Western was one of the earliest steamships to cross the Atlantic and sailed to New York in just 15 days instead of a month. The wharf was destroyed during the Blitz and remodelled in the early 1950s with electric cranes, flush roadways, railways and transit sheds to handle mixed cargo on ships from the Baltic and southern Ireland.

Prince's Wharf

Wapping Wharf

Prince's Wharf was the last to operate commercially when the Harbour closed in 1975. It is home to M Shed, a museum which tells of Bristol's place in the world. Narrow Quay and Broad Quay were the main trading wharves of the port for centuries until the expansion of Wapping wharf in the 1860s. Wapping Wharf further developed in the 1870's; this was open quayside with railway sidings. Steam trains run on the railway lines on specific days of the year.

The dry dock and the industrial buildings are the last remains of a shipyard that thrived on this site from 1820 until 1977. Launched in 1976, Miranda Guinness was the last ship built and also the world's first purpose-built beer tanker. When they closed, Charles Hill & Sons were the oldest shipbuilding company in the UK, having been established in 1772. The Albion Dockyard extended across the whole of what is now Bristol Marina. Boatbuilding and repair still continues here on a smaller scale.

Dry dock

Poole's Wharf

Merchants Dock was built in 1768 as Bristol's first wet dock and was operated by the Merchant Venturers. In return for wharfage, they built new quays and improved the facilities of the old. There is brick evidence of an old railway bridge. Poole's Wharf was established in 1772. Shipbuilding stopped in 1904, repairs continued until the 1930s. It became a coal-importing yard and home of the sand-dredging fleets. In 1991, the area was redeveloped with housing.

Baltic Wharf was once the home of several timber yards, where ships from the Baltics, Canada and Russia offloaded cargoes. Wharfs were not needed as the Dockers used the timber as gangplanks to and from the ships. The pub called the Cottage was once the office for one of the timber firms. The original building dates back to 1868. The old round-topped drying sheds are now used for the storage of boats and canoes.

The Cottage on Baltic Wharf

Quayside Residential Building

The quayside opposite the SS Great Britain was formerly called "The Mardyke" and was the area designated for ships to wait until they secured moorings. Capricorn Quay is the modern name for a residential development on the site of the Lime Kiln Dry Dock which closed in 1903. The grass area shows its outline. Porto Quay and Hanover quay stretch towards the Amphitheatre. Porto Quay was the last area to be named.

The old roofless large stone buildings are the last remaining structures of the Canon's Marsh Gas Works. This was Bristol's first gas works, initially making gas from whale oil in the 1820s but later converting to coal gas. The works remained active until the mid 1960s when natural gas arrived. The clean-up operation of the residual arsenic proved difficult, but now the buildings are being developed into apartments and duplexes.

Bathurst Wharf was constructed in the 1860s and was home to transit sheds and an oil seed mill. Now it is a pedestrianized residential area named Merchants Quay. The lock at the end led into Bathurst Basin and was created by enlarging the mill pond which had stood there since the middle Ages. Bathurst Basin, named after MP Charles Bathurst, could be used as a half-tidal basin. The river Malago flowed into the river Avon here prior to the basin being built.

Another lock led into the New Cut, used as an access by smaller vessels bypassing the main entrance to the Harbour. A new wharf was made by the coming of the Midland harbour railway. It was extended 400ft west of the Prince St Bridge. Opposition from GWR meant that Midland Railway stopped here. Midland Wharf was renamed Phoenix Wharf in the 1970s after the renovation work funded here by Phoenix Assurance. The entrance to Redcliffe Caves can be found here.

Old Bathhurst Lock

Old Railway
Lower Guinea Street

The railway connecting the docks to Temple Meads station came through a tunnel that ran underneath St Mary's churchyard and broke through the middle of Redcliffe caves. The railway crossed Bathurst lock on a steam powered bascule bridge, the site of the present footbridge, before continuing to Princes Wharf. Lucas Brothers used Redcliffe Wharf and traded in palm oil, a staple in the manufacture of soap. It is now a base for traditional boatbuilding.

The wharves known as Redcliffe Back and Welsh Back are one mile long, having a depth, which allows five hundred ton ships to dock. Welsh Back was where the Trows docked, that is, ships that sailed between Bristol and South Wales. Redcliffe Back was mainly the home to granaries and mills. The Backs are named because they were the backs of the rich merchants' houses. Alice Chester donated the first crane to the Welsh Back.

Towards Bristol Bridge, the wharf is damaged by a bomb hole dropped during World War II and is retained as a memorial. The Merchant Seamen's memorial commemorating those who lost their lives sailing from Bristol can also be found here. The dockside sheds of Buchannan's Wharf on Redcliffe Back have become bars, restaurants and chic little shops. The Western Counties Agricultural Society and Proctor Baker owned many of the buildings. These buildings have been transformed into flats.

Welsh Back bomb damage

Temple Back held a lead works, an iron foundry, a glass bottle works, a white lead works, a railway locomotive factory, a major railway bridge, a gas works and a soap factory. The façade of the Central Electric Lighting Station, opened in 1893, Bristol's first generating station for electric street lighting can be seen. As the railway grew so did the number of bridges needed to cross the river. They have been butted together to look like one large bridge.

Temple Back was badly bomb-damaged in the 1940's and was left as a wasteland. The 1960's concrete jungle which replaced some of the damaged buildings has now gone. These buildings and the wasteland area have been completely regenerated with stylish buildings. It is now a vibrant home to hotels, pubs, insurance and financial institutions, and has been rebranded as Temple Quay in the Bristol Enterprise zone.

Temple Back

Wapping Wharf

In August 1969 the Council was intending to withdraw navigation rights in the run-down Bristol Docks and fill in large sections. Following a public meeting, a protest was organised and, after much work by many local groups, a redevelopment plan was resolved, and so began the ongoing redevelopment of Hotwells, Canon's Marsh and Spike Island. Most of the redevelopment of bars, homes and businesses, has now been completed.

Bristol's harbourside renaissance began with the opening of the Arnolfini, in the 1970s. The 19th century two storey former tea warehouse, Bush House, became the Arnolfini centre for contemporary arts, with galleries, an auditorium, shop plus restaurant. Bristol's Arnolfini had had a nomadic early life until it found these permanent headquarters. This side of St Augustine's Reach is called Narrow Quay.

Arnolfini

Bordeaux Quay

The old warehouses and other buildings that line the quaysides have now all taken on new uses. New housing has been built along the waterfront. Dockside buildings and wharves have found new uses and exciting developments are in place. Some has become cafes and bars. The area has become a vibrant place to visit, especially during the summer months when various festivals take place. Bordeaux Quay is the new name for this side of St Augustine's Reach.

Canon's Marsh was an area of marshy hay meadow owned by St Augustine's Abbey. Rail connections were added in 1900 and the Great Western Railway used the site to house goods sheds. E Shed has a very ornate end and it was completed in 1896. Behind the baroque domed facade are shops, cafes and the Watershed Media Centre. Opened in 1982, it claims to be the United Kingdom's first dedicated media centre. Most of the Watershed is situated on the second floor of two of the sheds.

Watershed entrance

Refurbished in 2005, it houses three cinemas, a café/bar, events/conferencing spaces, and office spaces for administrative and creative staff. The building is currently host to Futurelab, UWE eMedia, and ArtsMatrix and annual film festivals, including ResFest, Depict!, Brief Encounters, the Lesbian and Gay Film Festival, Slapstick Film Festival, Wild Screen and online short-film festival. eShed.net is a showcase for digital art made by young people.

Lloyds bank has moved their headquarters to a prime harbour side location to continue Bristol's fine financial and insurance standing. Huge concrete bonded warehouses for tobacco were blown up in 1988 for the Lloyds Bank headquarters to begin. The area of dockside in front of the building is called the Amphitheatre. Interesting public squares and spaces with a collection of public art are all in close proximity, the area was developed as part of the @Bristol development for the millennium.

Amphitheatre

The Amphitheatre is used to stage events during the different festivals throughout the year. It has a capacity for a maximum of 10,000 visitors, staff and traders. The Amphitheatre takes its radius from the stone tower which was originally the base for a steam crane that was scrapped in 1969. The weather vane and turret were rescued from a demolished building elsewhere in the city and placed here in the 1970s.

In 1780 there had been nine shipyards in Bristol. There are still small boatyards and dry docks operating within the docks. At its height, the harbour had over 40 cranes for unloading ships. Only seven survive today. Brunel proved that larger ships could be more efficient and the restraints of the horseshoe bend on the river, the death knell was sounded for the city docks and the docks moved to the mouth of the river.

11 Seafaring Heritage.

The common seal of the burgesses of Bristol, engraved in the reign of Edward I (1272-1307) shows the early history of Bristol as a port. It is a merchant ship approaching the castle's Watergate along the River Avon, which teems with fish, including a large eel, the Latin legend translated as 'I am the key of the hidden port. The sailor watches the port side of the ship. The watchman points out the port with his finger.' This and other friezes can be seen on Broad Quay house, showing the history of Bristol.

A decade before Columbus, Bristol sailors had fished the cod-rich seas off Newfoundland and had landed to split, salt and dry their catches for transport back to Europe, particularly to Spain and Portugal. Columbus seems to have learned of Bristol's secret and in 1492 Columbus allegedly discovered the New World, a fact that the Bristol sailors disputed. A letter to Columbus pretty well clinches the matter. It reads, 'It is considered certain that the cape of the said land was discovered in the past by men from Bristol 'as your Lordship well knows'.

Replica of the Matthew

The name 'America' has been linked to that of Richard ap Merryk, also known as Ameryk, merchant and collector of custom dues for the Port of Bristol. In 1495 John Cabot and his three sons sailed to take possession in the King's name any lands they discovered. In 1497 Cabot set out from Bristol, financed by Ameryk and crossed the Atlantic Ocean in his ship 'The Matthew'. The New Found Land he discovered was the mainland of North America, on Midsummer's Day, 1497. Towers to Cabot can be found in both Bristol and Newfoundland.

Bristol has a rogues' gallery of reckless, vicious pirates but none of them approach the infamous Blackbeard. He hailed from Redcliffe and his real name was Edward or Edmund Teach. He terrorized shipping, was responsible for more than 2,000 deaths during his reign. He was the most bloodthirsty of all pirates in the early 18th century. He wore a long black beard and during assaults on ships he thrust smoking fuses into his beard and matted hair. He met a violent death on the coast of Carolina, murdered by pirate-hunters.

In 1708 Woodes Rogers began his first voyage in his ship, The Duke. In 1709 he stopped at an island and discovered Alexander Selkirk, who had been shipwrecked and lived on the island for nearly four and a half years. As a privateer Woodes Rogers' acquired a considerable amount of money. He was made governor of Bahamas in 1716 and cleared it of pirates by a mixture of pardoning, bribes and punitive action. He died in Queen Square in 1732 and there is a plaque on the present building.

The largest was the SS Great Britain. This iconic steam ship was designed by Isambard Kingdom Brunel, and lies at the heart of a multi award-winning visitor attraction. It was the first ship to be built of iron. Brunel rejected using conventional paddlewheels and gave the SS Great Britain a screw propeller. This innovative liner was launched in 1843 and was 322 ft long, 51 ft wide and the screw propeller was 15'6" in diameter, the ship had six masts to assist the engines or to propel should the engines fail.

The Great Britain's rusting hulk was abandoned in the Falkland Islands towards the end of the 19th century. Brought back to the Great Western Dock in 1970, the ship has undergone extensive and dedicated restoration. The hull is now enclosed in glass, made to look like water, to preserve the ironworks and now attracts thousands of visitors each year. Brunel created a ship that changed history, paving the way for the large ocean liners of today.

Even though the Floating Harbour removed the tidal problem in Bristol city docks, boats became larger and it was difficult for them to negotiate the River Avon. It is five miles from the Docks to the Severn. Many ships ran aground negotiating the Horseshoe Bend and rocky outcrops. The most famous victim was the Demerara, built in Bristol as a paddle steamer in 1851 and was the world's second largest ship. She was launched in Bristol on 27th September 1851 and wrecked on 10th November through careless navigation. The Demerara was declared a loss by her underwriters. Only a replica of her figurehead still remains on a building next to the Hippodrome.

Bristolian Samuel Plimsoll, was born at 9 Colston Parade, Redcliffe in 1824. He became a Liberal politician, keenly interested in safety at sea. Plimsoll wrote a book called 'Our Seamen' in 1873 which condemned the ship owners who risked sailors' lives by dangerously overloading their vessels with cargo. Plimsoll died in 1898. To mark Samuel Plimsoll's achievement in making ships safer, a bust of him was erected at the side of the river Avon by the Cumberland Basin. Thousands of commuters passed by it each day, without giving it a second glance. After five years in storage it has been moved and can now be seen in the harbourside, at Capricorn quay.

12 Slavery.

Bristol, before the Normans invaded, was a slaving centre; the city ran a thriving business in white slavery. Captives from Wales and regions of England were brought here to be bought and sold, many shipped to the ready market in Viking Dublin. William the Conqueror clamped down on slave trading. It was banned altogether in 1102. When Henry II conquered Ireland, English slaves throughout Ireland were restored to freedom, given trade and residential rights in Dublin in 1172, making it, for a period, almost a colony of Bristol.

At the end of the 17th century an organization of elite merchants in Bristol, who managed Bristol's harbour, called The Society of Merchant Venturers wanted to participate in the lucrative African slave trade. Between 1697 and 1807, 2,108 known ships left Bristol to make the trip to Africa and onwards across the Atlantic with slaves. The Society of Merchant Venturers managed the harbour until the early 19th century. It is still a society today.

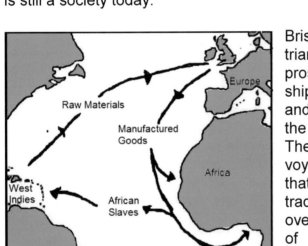

Bristol was one of the three points of the slave triangle, already a wealthy city, the city prospered even more. In Bristol there were the ship owners, merchants, slave-ship captains and crew. The ship owners invested money in the slaving voyages and provided the ships. The merchants invested money in the slaving voyages, by equipping the ship and the goods that were traded with Africa. The roles of slave traders, ship owners, and merchants often overlapped. At its peak it is estimated that 60% of Bristolians were directly or indirectly associated with this dreadful trade.

Pero's Bridge

The Georgian House, at No 7, Great George Street is an example of a six storey town house from about 1796. It was built for John Pinney, a plantation owner and sugar merchant. It is one of the most complete 18th century town houses surviving in the UK. It is now a museum with decoration and furniture true to the period. In the harbour, Pero's Bridge is in honour of the slave of John Pinney. The two large horns are counter-balances for the centre section that opens to let boats through.

Edward Colston's wealth was acquired through the trade and exploitation of slaves. In 1683 he is listed as a West India merchant who traded primarily in St Kitts. He was a member of the Royal African Company. He owned a large fleet of ships trading in sugar and a sugar refinery by St Peter's Church. Until 1992 three charities were in existence set up by Colston, The Colston Society, The Dolphin Society and the Anchor Society. The Merchants' impact on the city was enormous. They founded Bristol University, a navigation school and Bristol's first water supply company. They donated half of the Downs to the city, paid for the Suspension Bridge to be built, and financed the Great Western Railway.

The Navigation School was founded in 1595; this in turn became Merchant Venturers' College in 1894, then later Bristol Polytechnic before it's reincarnation as UWE. In 1708 Edward Colston founded Colston's School and appointed the Merchant Venturers as managers. Colston's Girls' School was created in 1891. Today the Merchants sponsor the Merchants' Academy in Withywood, which replaced the Community School.

Royal Fort

Other buildings that have slavery connections include the Royal Fort, which was extended by Thomas Tyndall in about 1767 on the site of the Royal Fort precinct which had been built during the English Civil War in the 1640s to protect the city from the roundheads. Its three facades have three different classical styles: Baroque, Palladian and Rococo, after three separate architects had submitted designs. The finished wooden architect's model survives in the house.

Other buildings were Redland Court, owned by Sir Robert Yeamans in the 1680s. There are African heads carved in stone on the back of Redland Chapel. Also, Ashton Court has a long history dating back to medieval times. The mansion and stables are a Grade I listed building and have 850 acres of woodland and grassland. The lower lodge and attached gates, railings and bollards are Grade II* listed. Its owner, Jarrid Smyth was involved in the slave trade.

Ashton Court

In the early years Quakers were involved, both owning slave ships and sugar plantations. By the 1760s they began to campaign against the trade and went on to be leaders of the Abolitionist movement with reformers such as Mary Carpenter, Hannah More, William Wilberforce and Thomas Clarkson, speaking out against the slave trade and boycotting West Indian sugar in 1778. The landlord of The Seven Stars pub in St Thomas St helped Thomas Clarkson investigate the Slave Trade.

Charles Wesley

It was normal for up to a quarter of any crew and its prisoners to die from illness and disease during the voyage. Clarkson was the president of the world's first human rights organization which is now called Anti-Slavery International. Opposition to the slave trade gained momentum during the late 18th century. The trade was abolished in British territories in 1807. Throughout 2007, Bristol played a leading role in the national commemoration Abolition 200, to mark the anniversary of the Abolition of the Slave Trade Act. Events and exhibitions took place throughout the year, including Charles Wesley's 300th birthday celebrations and the St Paul's Carnival which celebrated its 40th anniversary.

13 Bristol, the City of Churches.

Bristol was known as the City of Churches, with 12 churches within the old city wall.

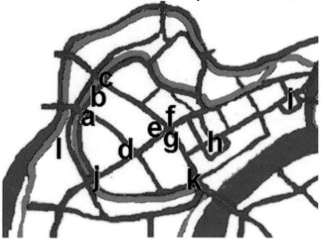

Within the walls
a St Giles
b St Lawrence
c St John
d St Werburgh
e St Ewan
f Christ Church
g All Saints
h St Mary-le-Port
i St Peter
j St Leonard
k St Nicholas
l St Stephen

Town and Castle Walls
Streets and Paths

Christ Church, which had existed for hundreds of years on this Wine Street/Broad Street corner, was demolished in the 18th century and a new church built. The nearby church of St Ewan in Corn Street had been closed, (it was pulled down in 1820 for the Old Council House) so the names were combined to form Christ Church with St Ewans. The brightly coloured Quarter Jacks are a survival from the original church, and these jacks strike on every quarter hour.

Not many of the 12 churches now remain. Some of the old churches are used for other purposes, but others still remain as active places of worship. St Werburgh's church originally stood in Corn Street. The building caused the road to narrow, and larger horse-drawn carriages were causing congestion. In 1878, it was not in use as a church and was demolished for road widening. The tower and some other sections were removed and rebuilt stone by stone to the area now known as St Werburgh's after the church. Decommissioned for use as a church in the 1980s it is now an indoor climbing centre. It has been designated on the National Heritage List for England as a Grade II* listed building.

Middle Ages guilds were an important feature of town life; each had its own patron saint and was associated with different crafts. The religious guild of Kalendars, composed of clergy and laity, met on or near the kalends (the first day of the month) and was in existence by 1147. At first it met in Trinity church, later moving to All Saints (pictured). The guild had four permanent chantry priests. The priests lived in a house next to All Saints church. The house was rebuilt in 1443. It had a free access library in an attic above the north aisle of All Saints. The prior maintained the library, gave a weekly public lecture, and explained the scriptures to any who asked. The guild dissolved in 1548.

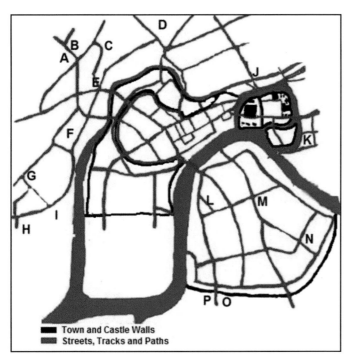

Town and Castle Walls
Streets, Tracks and Paths

Outside the Walls

A St Michael
B St Mary Magalene Nunnery
C Fransican Friary
D St James Priory
E St Bartholomew's Hospital
F Camelite Friary
G St Mary & St Mark
H St Augustine's Monastry
I St Augustine the Less
J Dominican Friary
K St Philip's Priory
L St Thomas
M Temple Church
N Eremites Priory
O St Mary Redcliffe
P St John's Hospital

Some of the churches outside the city wall belonged to abbeys or priories. A lot of these became parish churches at the Reformation.

In the 16th Century Bristol comprised of 17 parishes, each with its own parish church. Closely clustered together in the old city, the many spires and towers of the churches can still be seen from a distance. Four of these churches still cluster close together at the top of Corn Street, in the oldest part of the city; these being Christ Church with St Ewan, All Saints, St Mary-Le-Port and St Nicholas. Over the years some of the churches have been demolished, others were destroyed or damaged during WW2 and one was moved elsewhere in the city, leaving the above and St John, St Peter and St Stephen standing.

Excavations in 1975 suggest that St Peters was the site of Bristol's first church and that it was a minster of the 8th century. St Peter's has Saxon foundations, has a 12th century lower tower, the rest of the church being built in the 15th century. St Peter's lay outside the walls of Saxon Bristol. The 12th century city wall runs under the west end of the present church. When the Castle was demolished in 1646, the church nearly suffered the same fate until the arrival of Prince Rupert saved it from destruction.

Bristol Cathedral is on a site that has probably had a church on it for over a thousand years. The Abbey of St Augustine was completed in 1165 and centuries later, in 1542, it was rededicated as The Cathedral Church of the Holy and Undivided Trinity. It became the Cathedral Church of the Diocese of Bristol with the dissolution of the monasteries, when Bristol gained city status from Henry VIII, to go with the county status of 1373.

The Chapter House in the Cathedral has one of the finest examples of Norman Rooms in the world and has not changed much since it was completed. The cathedral has much of interest, including unique architectural features, unusual memorials and an historic organ. Bristol Cathedral is a grade I listed building. The Cathedral was conceived as a hall church, and it also has three unique vaults. The vaulted ceilings in the nave, choir, and aisles are all at the same height. There is a brick-lined 19th Century burial vault under the floor of the Eastern Lady Chapel

Bristol is also home to the Roman Catholic Cathedral Church of SS. Peter and Paul and is known as Clifton Cathedral. The Cathedral was consecrated on 29 June 1973, replacing a wooden-framed pro-Cathedral of the Holy Apostles that had been built in the mid-19th century. It can group 1,000 people closely around the high altar. The arrangement of the Blessed Sacrament Chapel and the Baptismal Font in relationship to the movement of people entering and leaving determined the shape of the building. It was granted grade 2 listed building status in 2000. A copper tube containing plans of the cathedral and other items were buried under the foundation stone.

St. Mary Redcliffe is Bristol's largest parish church and has the second tallest spire in the country. In 1574, Queen Elizabeth I is said to have proclaimed the Parish Church to be the "fairest, goodliest and most famous parish church in England." In 1446 its spire was struck by lightning and two thirds of it fell. The church tower then stayed in a truncated state until the 1860s, when a new 87m (285ft) high spire was built. A tramline lies embedded in the churchyard after a bombing raid during WWII.

St Mary and St Marks, The Lord Mayor's Chapel has stood since 1230 AD and it is all that remains of the Hospital of St Mark which was founded by Maurice de Gaunt, in 1220, to feed the poor and care for the sick. In 1540 Henry VIII seized it and the City fathers purchased the buildings and lands from him, as the City needed a place for its public functions. It is the only municipal chapel in England. The Lord Mayor's Chapel lies north-east to south-west. Churches are built on an east-west alignment and deviations from that pattern are very rare.

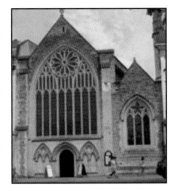

During the blitz four of Bristol's ancient churches, St Peter's, the interior of St Nicholas, St Mary-le-Port and Temple Church (pictured) were badly damaged. The St James' Presbyterian Church of England was gutted. When St Mary-le-Port was bombed in 1940, the tower formed a chimney for the resulting fire and the heat was so intense that it melted the bells down the walls. The metal is supposed to survive to this day.

The City of Churches had in one night become the city of ruins. St Peters had the oldest church bell in Bristol. The bell was sent to Canada following the blitz. The church is maintained as a poignant dedicatory of the last war and the names of all Bristol civilians killed in the Blitz are on a memorial on the church wall. All that remains of St Mary-le-Port (pictured) is the 15th century tower, a grade II listed building. It is hidden away behind the now disused Bristol branch of the Bank of England. The word Port could mean a gate, a market, or a port. Here the meaning was clearly market. St Mary in the market lay between the old wooden fort and the minster of St Peter's which lay within its own precinct.

The third bombed church was St Nicholas. It is unique in that the clock face in Baldwin Street has three hands, an hour, a minute and a second hand. The original clock was installed in the early 19th Century. The seconds hand was added during renovation in the 1870s. The clockwork mechanism was destroyed in 1940 but it was repaired and converted to electricity. St Nicholas currently houses private city council offices.

St Thomas was completed in 1793. The church survived the "Bristol Blitz" of the Second World War, but most of the buildings surrounding it were destroyed. The congregation declined after the war and the church was finally declared redundant. The last service was held there at Christmas 1982. This was a parish full of rich clothiers. It is in the care of the Churches Conservation Trust. The building is currently leased to a Romanian Orthodox Church community who use it for worship on Sundays and special days. It is recorded in the National Heritage List for England as a designated Grade II* listed building.

The government wanted to knock down Temple Church after the war because of the leaning tower. The lean of the tower developed within a short time of its construction, due to being built on marshy land. The foundations were strengthened and a further section added to the tower, which leans in a different direction. The original church was built by the Knights Templar who was a society of soldier-monks formed during the time of the Crusades. It included a Weavers' Chapel which contained much painted glass. After the bombing it was deconsecrated. The ruins are now looked after by English Heritage.

St James Priory next to the bus station is the oldest building in Bristol still in use today. Robert Fitzroy founded the Priory in 1129, at the same time as rebuilding the castle and developing the town into a major provincial capital. In the medieval period it was home to Benedictine monks. In the Middle Ages it was a major landowner to the north and east. The Priory was dissolved and many of its buildings were demolished. Only the west end survived as a smaller parish church.

Bristol was a centre for non-conformists. Two churches remain in Broadmead, John Wesley's new room and the Baptist church. Dorothy Hazzard was a religious reformer and during the defence of the city during the Royalist siege led a group of 200 women who tried to seal the Frome Gate. She testified at the trial of Nathaniel Fiennes who had surrendered Bristol to the Royalists. She challenged the religious thinking of the time.

Unitarian church Brunswick Square

These were the beginnings of Broadmead Baptist Church, the first dissenting church in Bristol, formed in 1640. There has been a Baptist church in the heart of the city of Bristol, since then. The church was founded by five individuals for the right to worship according to conscience. The original Baptist church was enlarged and rebuilt several times up to 1877. Now a modern building on the first and second floor, it is known as the church above the shops.

Brothers John and Charles Wesley lived and preached in Bristol and campaigned for the abolition of slavery. Charles was a hymn writer of great renown; his most famous work is Hark the Herald Angels. The New Room is the world's first and oldest surviving Methodist building built in 1739. The chapel itself is on the ground floor and is accessible from either the Broadmead or Horsefair courtyards. Upstairs, are the Preachers' Rooms, where the museum can be found.

Quakers arrived in Bristol in 1654. Quakers Friars was built in 1670 on the site of the Dominican Friary. The Society of Friends were persecuted, imprisoned and as 'non-freemen' they were not allowed to carry out any trade or commerce in the City. Cutlers' and Bakers' Halls, were acquired in 1845. . It became Bristol Registry Office and now a restaurant. The Stoke Bishop district does not have a public house as Quakers lived in this area. The Friends Meeting House moved to Champion Square in 1962.

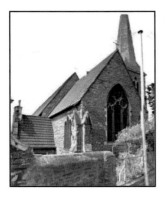At the last census there were about forty five religions being practised in Bristol. The other most established are the Unitarians, Polish Roman Catholics, Eastern Orthodox Church, New Life Church, Bhuddism, Hindu, Muslim, Hebrew, Sikh, Jehovah's Witnesses, Rastafarian and Greek Orthodox Church. The Greek Orthodox Church (pictured) in Baptist Mills started renting St Simons in 1958. In 1963 the church was renamed to Apostles St Peter and Paul, after which the congregation bought the building. The church wall is made from blocks made out of black Copper slag.

14 Industrial Heritage.

The industrial revolution brought factories, potteries and glassworks. The slave-produced goods such as sugar and tobacco, grown on the European owned plantations, and cotton were shipped to Bristol and provided new industries and markets for the city. The modern industries included sugar refining, tobacco processing, snuff making, cocoa and chocolate making, wine bottling, and the making of fine glass, porcelain and pottery, engineering, chemicals, furniture and soap making. The metal industry made brass, zinc, lead and iron goods including cannons, chains and anchors.

The main brewery was the firm of Georges & Co., which in 1788 took control of the Bristol Porter Brewery. It already had a large share of the Bristol market when in 1888 it acquired limited company status. In 1919 the Company purchased the extensive premises originally known as the Talbot Hotel, at the corner of Victoria Street and Bath Street. In this building the offices of the Company were situated.

By the 1920s Georges had more than 700 tied houses in the Bristol region. More mergers followed, until in 1962, having acquired a local monopoly, Georges itself became victim to a takeover by Courage. In 1999 the brewery ceased to brew, and beer production on the site ceased after 210 years. Parts of the original building still exist in the today. Some public houses still show signage of Georges & Co.

The Bristol region was one of the first places to use coal as a fuel in industrial applications. First it was used in soap manufacture and then in glass making, brewing, pottery and in many other ways. The Bristol area had ample reserves of coal and most of these lay to the east of the city the rest were in south Bristol. There had been small scale production in Kingswood for centuries, the earliest record shows licenses issued in the 13th century. The emergence of the steam engine meant that not only did demand increase dramatically but there was also the power to move it to where it was wanted.

Production from the Bristol coalfield greatly increased over much of the nineteenth century, reaching a peak in the 1870s, after that it steadily declined. The South Liberty pit delivered its final ton of coal in the 1920s whilst the Speedwell Colliery was the last pit to close in 1939. On Troopers Hill there is evidence in the shape of the land of mine shafts that are likely to date from the 1700s. The names of some villages, public houses and the chimney or stack that still stands at the junction of Troopers Hill Road and Crews Hole Road is all that remains of these collieries. Originally the chimney was at the corner of the engine house and parts of the walls of that building can still be seen. The corners of the stack are formed with black copper slag blocks. This structure is also Grade II listed.

FIRE ENGINE

Cattybrook Brick Works was founded in 1865 when engineer Charles Richardson, was impressed by the quality of the clay being dug out of Patchway Tunnel. The brickworks went on to supply 74,400,000 bricks for the Severn Tunnel. Most of the bricks were red in colour, but Yellow, buff and blue bricks were also produced. The character of many buildings in Bristol such as The Fish Market (pictured), owes much to the combination of red and yellow Cattybrook bricks. The Brickworks is still operated at Almondsbury by Ibstock Bricks.

Glass was a major Bristol industry. Old prints of the city show at least 15 glass cones using local coal, limestone and red leads. Hotwell Spa needed bottles, and there was a big demand for windows from the new Georgian city of Bath. Harvey's Bristol Cream sherry sold its world famous sherry in blue bottles, the blue colour comes from cobalt, a metal mined in Saxony. Bristol was the main import centre so cobalt glass was named Bristol Blue - no matter where it was made. The sandstone was mined in the man-made Redcliffe Caves during the 15 to 18 century, extending some 2-3 acres under the City. The extensive cave system can be accessed by appointment. These caves were later used as warehouses to store ships' cargoes.

Bristol's glassworkers were also world-famous for fine cut and engraved glass. Bristol's last flint glasshouse closed in 1851 and the last bottle-house in 1823. One glass cone survives as the base of the Glass Kiln restaurant, next to St Mary Redcliffe church. It was truncated in the 1930s when the upper structure became dangerous. Bristol Blue is being made by hand using techniques of 200 years ago. There is more Bristol Blue being made today than there was in its heyday.

The sugar houses produced fine white sugar from the dark brown sugar imported from the plantations. There were 20 sugar houses in the city. Sugar started out as a luxury item but by the late eighteenth century an increasing number used it to sweeten tea, cocoa and in the production of rum. Steam engines were developed to speed up sugar production. A boiler room, engine house & chimney, were added. The remaining sugar house in Lewin's Mead is Grade II listed.

The sugar refinery processed the molasses by removing the impurities. They produced various grades of pure white crystalline sugar. The sugar was moulded in to conical loaves of sugar and you can see an example of a sugar loaf and sugar tongs on the pub sign and in the kitchen of the Georgian House Museum. It closed as a refinery in 1831 after which it continued to be put to a wide range of industrial uses.

Fire was a hazard in the sugar refining industry; between 1670 and 1859 no less than 11 sugar houses were destroyed by fire. Due to the high insurance premiums, sugar merchants started their own insurance firms, the first being the Bristol Fire Office founded in 1718 which by 1837 was absorbed into the Sun Fire Office. This was the Bristol's only fire service until the Police Fire Brigade Service was formed in 1877. The nearby pub gets its name from the sugar refinery that burned down in 1859.

In the early 18th century Bristol was second only to London in decorative ware. Production of delftware began at Brislington around 1652. The first pottery in the city started in 1683, at Temple Backs. In the early 18th century production spread to Limekiln Lane and Redcliff Back, as well as a number of smaller potteries. By 1777 only the Temple Backs pottery remained and this changed to creamware production now known as Pountney & Co. Under-glaze transfer printing at Bristol was in use by about 1825.

Some of the Bristol Series (Avon Series) views are very rare. The Thames series uses the same borders as the Bristol. Poultney's reproduced both the Bristol and Thames views in the 20th century. In 1905 the business moved to Fishponds, It was the most modern pottery in Europe at the time. Production was in a single-story building, raw materials entering one end and finished products leaving the other, where it continued until 1969.

The Royal Cauldron name was acquired in 1962 but the company went bankrupt in 1971. On closure the copper plates and the pattern books were destroyed, ending over 300 years of Bristol decorative pottery. Stoneware was produced from the late 17th century until 1940. William Powell developed a stoneware glaze, which eventually replaced salt-glazing. Powell and Price were major makers of stoneware bottles such as oil jars, pickling pots, pitchers and mugs.

The Bristol Fire Clay Company made sanitary ware, chimney pots, fire bricks, tiles, etc. Other companies made redware pipes for flues, hot air, draining and flower pots, as well as bricks. Cookworthy's hard-paste porcelain business transferred to Bristol in 1770, but the factory closed in 1781. After closure the pottery was taken over and clay pipes for tobacco smoking were made there. The remaining stock of porcelain was still being sold in 1783.

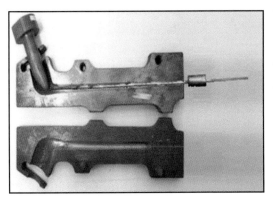

Clay pipes had been made in the City from at least 1617 and a guild of pipe makers founded in 1652. Long pipes were set at 16 inches. During the early 18th century tobacco became cheaper, and the bowls of pipes became larger. Thomas George & Co. closed in 1921. Pipes were made in iron or brass moulds, each mould having a life of about 10 years. Bristol pipes were generally of a superior quality, with elaborate mouldings, and many of them have makers' marks.

Lead was mined in the nearby Mendip hills and of poor quality, as it was hardened by the presence of arsenic. It was unsuitable for pipes or sheets for roofing but was ideal for shot and bullets. The tall chimney in Millennium Square is one of the few survivors of the large number of works that existed in the first half of the 20th century. It housed Rowe Bros lead works, built in the late 1890s to take advantage of the railway that was about to arrive here.

William Watts patented a new method of making lead shot. Watts simply poured the molten lead through a zinc sieve, it emerged in drops, which fell, hardening, into a vat of water, where they were preserved as near-perfect spheres. The first shot tower in the world was built in Cheese Lane but was demolished for road widening in 1968. Bristol's first brick-built building was replaced by a 140-foot tall reinforced concrete landmark. Sheldon Bush, the last lead manufacturer, closed in 1995, but the tower, a Grade II listed building and one of only three shot towers left in the country, is still there and will be preserved as part of Bristol's skyline.

The earliest reference to a man smoking in England was in 1556, incidentally the man was from the port of Bristol. The leaf tobacco, also imported from the plantations, was made into smokable twists of tobacco or snuff for sniffing. The tobacco industry in Bristol started in 1786 when Wills, Watkins & Co. was founded by Henry Overton Wills and his partner Watkins. Through name changes and various mergers it finally became WD & HO Wills in 1830.

Brands such as passing clouds, Gold Flake, three castles, wild woodbines and Cinderella were launched. 1901 saw the formation of The Imperial Tobacco Company. In 1887, Wills were one of the first UK tobacco companies to include advertising cards in their packs of cigarettes. They pioneered canteens for the workers, free medical care, sports facilities and paid holidays. 'No. 1' Factory was in East Street 'No. 3' in Raleigh Road and No. 4 in Ashton Gate.

From 1930 through to the early 60's Castella Panatela cigars, Strand, and Embassy cigarettes were introduced, and tipped Woodbine, Capstan Medium and Gold Flake. WD & HO Wills imported large quantities and stored it in the red brick buildings bonded tobacco. A Bond was finished in 1905, followed by B Bond in 1908. The third was delayed by the WW1; the fourth one was never built. B bond now houses the create centre and the Bristol Record Office.

Bonded Warehouses

The last of the Wills family retired in 1969. In 1974 the first cigarettes were produced at the new Hartcliffe Factory, soon to become the company's Head Office. The Hanson Trust took over Imperial Tobacco Limited in 1986, the 200th anniversary of W.D. & H.O. Wills. In 1990 a new cigar factory in Winterstoke Road, Ashton was built. In 1999 the Hartcliffe factory was demolished, ending cigarette production in Bristol.

The large factory and warehouse buildings remain prominent buildings in Bristol, although much of the existing land and buildings have been converted to other uses. The Tobacco Factory (pictured) in Raleigh Road now houses a theatre, restaurant and bar but was formerly the site of the Imperial Tobacco Research Department. The facade of cigar factory in Winterstoke Road, Ashton remains and is part of a new headquarters for Imperial Tobacco.

W.D. & H.O. Wills was not the only tobacco company. Four tobacco companies merged to become Edwards, Ringer & Biggs. Franklyn, Davey & Co had set up before 1779 in Welsh Back, and William Ringer in the High Street in 1813. Over the years WD Bigg & Co and WH Edwards merged to form the new company. The company was then established in Redcliffe Street site. The site closed in 1974.

Kleeneze homecare started in a Bristol broom cupboard in 1923. The business moved into their Hanham factory in 1928 making brushes which were sold door-to-door by salesmen. Between 1945 and 1980, the range of products expanded. The Kleeneze agents were self-employed, running and owning their own home shopping businesses. In the 1990's the company helped to found the Direct Selling Association. Between 2004 and 2006, Kleeneze expanded into Holland and Germany. Kleeneze was bought by Findel PLC in 2007 and moved to a state-of-the-art office and warehouse facility in Accrington.

E. S. & A. Robinson was founded in 1844 making paper bags for grocery stores. Progressing onto tradesman's almanac, elaborate notepapers and bound ledgers. It held the greatest supply of paper for any firm in the kingdom. They bought the rights to a patent for a paper satchel bag, which allowed paper packaging of materials such as Portland Cement and flour. Mass production of the carton and folding boxes followed. At the turn of the century, bags printed with logos and advertising became a hit.

Strachan Henshaw Machinery manufactured paper handling and printing equipment. In 1879 the company made the first ever automatic paper bag-making machine. In WW1 the factory made munitions. The company was acquired by Robinsons in 1920 but remained separate. In 1950s it developed the first paperback book press with rubber printing plates and a low cost inking system which allowed books to be produced inexpensively. It closed in 2000.

E. S. & A. Robinson opened a cardboard box factory in 1922 and a waxed paper factory in 1929. In World War II the company's aircraft components reproduction process that was adopted by practically the whole of the British aircraft industry. Robinson's merged to become the Dickson Robinson Group in 1966; the brands included Sellotape and Basildon Bond. In 1989 DRG was acquired through a leverage buyout. Various other buyouts followed and the factory finally closed in 1996.

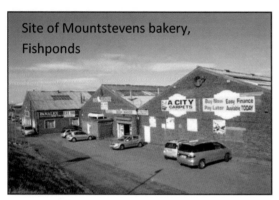

Site of Mountstevens bakery, Fishponds

Mountstevens was founded in 1911 and the first shop opened in St Marks Road. The bakery remained in family hands for 86 years and had more than 90 bakery shops and coffee houses across the south and west of England. The bakery was sold in 1997 to Lyndale Food, then to Cleary Foods in 2001. In 2002 the bakery closed, with the loss of 800 jobs. The bakery in Fishponds Trading Estate now has other uses.

William Proctor Baker became a partner in his father's business in 1860. The Mill and granary in Buchanans Wharf was built in 1883-84, it is a grade II listed building and has now been transformed into flats. The company became one of the largest flour businesses in England. He became Bristol Lord Mayor 1871, was chairman of the Docks Committee and President of the General Hospital until his death in 1907.

Buchanans Wharf

In 1889 the business became Spillers and Bakers. In 1919 its title was changed into Spillers Milling and Associated Industries, then Spillers Limited in 1927. The company moved its Bristol works to Avonmouth in 1937. In 1979 by taken over by Dalgety plc. Spillers' flour milling operations were sold to Kerry Group plc in 1997. Kerry Group operations are now locally based at Portbury docks.

Henry Jones established a bakery in 39 and 37 Broadmead. He patented self-raising flour in 1845. By the end of 1846 its success led to him being appointed purveyor of patent flour and biscuits to Queen Victoria. He was granted a patent in the USA on 1 May 1849. His flour meant that hard tack could be removed from sailors of the British Navy. In 1855, his flour was approved at the behest of Florence Nightingale. His original formula is basically the same as that used by the company today, which is now owned by Kerry Foods Ltd. Hooks Mill, Boiling Wells Road, was owed by the Jones Family

Another baker was GA Witts and Sons that made the Wonderloaf. It was sold in waxed paper wrappers in a different colour for each day of the week. If it's fresher than Wonderloaf, it's still in the oven! The office building on Ashley Hill was once a girl's orphan asylum. The bread factory was behind this.

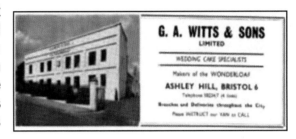

William Bonney moved from London and in 1695 was granted the right to establish a printing press as long as he exercised no other trade than that of printer. Prior to this, trades were restricted to the citizens of the city. This was the first printing press outside London. In Tower Street he printed essays, then in 1702 moved to Small Street and produced the first single sheet newspaper called the Bristol Post Boy. The publication lasted until 1715. Samuel Farley set up a rival, the Bristol Post Man, this lasted until 1725.

Edward Everard was a founder member of the Bristol Master Printers' and Allied Trades' Association and was the official printer to the Bristol Stock Exchange. In 1900 his printing works moved to new premises in Broad Street with an Art Nouveau frontage. At the top there is a lamp and mirror to symbolise light and truth. Below is Johann Gutenberg, father of printing, and William Morris, reviver of craftsmanship. In between the Spirit of Light spreads wings over arched windows. Everard's name in the Art Nouveau typeface he designed. The printing works closed in 1967 and the building narrowly escaped demolition in 1970 but the facade was preserved as it has the largest decorative facade of its kind in Britain. It has been designated by English Heritage as a grade II* listed building.

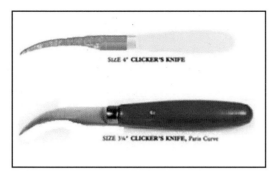

The footwear trade grew up as a result of coal mining. There were at least 119 in operation in 1901 and were very small concerns, producing for local or regional markets. Clickers cut out the leather. In 1880 G.B. Britton and George Jeffries built a small factory in Waters Road, Kingswood. The building contained treadle-operated sewing machines and crude presses for cutting out soles and insoles.

The uppers and bottoms were issued to out-workers who lasted, attached and finished the men's nailed boots in their own homes. The WW1 output was mainly army boots. G. B. Britton & Sons continued to expand and in 1930 the employment of out-workers ended, the production instead being made by machinery in the factory. Again in 1939 the company secured a contract for a substantial quantity of army boots.

The TUF boot was produced in 1955 and orders far exceeded production. The company was producing nearly 50,000 pairs of boots and shoes a week. In the 1930s GB Britton's employed 10,000 workers, but by 2001 only 130 workers were left. Shoe-making in Bristol came to an end with the closure of the footwear factory, it was then owned by UK Safety of Northampton

In 1192 soap makers were in Bristol, by 1562 there were more than 180, causing a production smell as it used rendered animal fat. There were two types "Bristol soap" and "Bristol grey soap". In 1632 a patent was granted to the Society of Soapmakers of Westminster. However production in Bristol was restricted to 600 tons per annum. Christopher Thomas & Bros made Puritan soap from 1745 to the take-over by Lever Bros in 1912, until closure in 1953. Gardiner Haskins now use the factory as their independent home store.

In 1872 HW Carter purchased the mineral water and cordial works of George Withy and Co and started making citrus fruit based drinks. Dr. Vernon Charley developed research using a pectinase enzyme process into pure fruit syrups. The drink was launched in 1936 under the name Ribena. During the Second World War, oranges and lemons quickly became in short supply. Blackcurrant cultivation was encouraged and from 1942, was made into blackcurrant syrup, almost all of it manufactured by Carters. It was distributed to the nation's children for free without the Ribena brand name, giving rise to the lasting popularity of blackcurrant flavourings in Britain. Production was moved to the Forest of Dean, where it is still made today.

Fry's was the oldest chocolate firm in Britain, and possibly in the world. Cocoa was mixed with flavourings and sugar in copper or tin pans, and then shaped into tablets. The tablets were put in a cup and hot water or milk was added. The Quaker Joseph Fry was able to adapt the inventions and experience of others for use in his own business. In 1776, one pound of Fry's famous chocolate retailed at 7/6d (35p), a sum only slightly below the average agricultural labourer's weekly wage.

In 1777, Fry's chocolate factory moved to the newly constructed Union Street premises. The company went on to have eight plants in Bristol. Fry's Chocolate Creams, was first introduced in 1853. In 1902, when milk chocolate was introduced, the Five Boys image became irretrievably connected with the famous bar. Turkish Delight followed in 1914, Crunchie in 1919 and the first UK chocolate egg, in 1873

J.S. Fry & Sons Ltd merged their financial interests with Cadbury in 1919. Chocolate and confectionery have been made on the Cadbury Somerdale site in Keynsham near Bristol since the 1930s and was still making chocolate on the outskirts of Bristol until Kraft Foods became the owners in 2010 and closed down the factory moving production to Poland.

Monsieur Guilbert, a Swiss Chocolatier, opened his first store on Park Street in 1910. During WWII the store was bombed and Guilbert's moved to Gloucester Road. In 1958 Guilbert's moved to Leonard Lane, now the home of the Craft Centre. Re-branding and expansion has meant another move for Guilbert's, and it has opened its new shop/ factory at the famous Foster rooms. It's believed to be the oldest Bristol building still in commercial use.

It was the home of the 15th Century merchant and Lord Mayor, John Foster. Every chocolate and fondant is still handmade and hand dipped, with the only difference of silicon moulds being used. Today they produce white, milk and dark chocolate bars and boxes of assorted creams, fondants, truffles and nuts. Guilbert kept the business for only some 10 or 15 years before selling it. Yet the name has stayed for over a 100 years of making chocolates.

Packer & Co started in 1881 in Easton. By 1901 a new factory was built at Greenbank. It was bought out in 1964 and renamed Cavenham Confectionery. The Elizabeth Shaw business was acquired in 1968 and Carsons Chocolate Company was later added. The Famous Names range of liqueur chocolates was launched in 1966. Between 1981 and 1991 the company changed hands four times. In 2000 saw a management buyout. In 2006 the Greenbank factory closed down, bringing to the end of an era spanning more than 100 years.

Bristol is still producing chocolate in the City. Apart from established company Guiberts there is a new company called Zara's Chocolates which started in 2011. It is possible to visit the shop in North Street, to watch her hand-making all the delicious chocolates. Or take part in a workshop to learn more about the art of the chocolatier

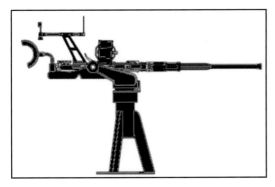

Webers chocolates were opened in 1914. In 1941 the factory was taken over by Thrissells Engineering and by January 1942 they were manufacturing breech casings and barrels for Oerlikon 20mm cannons. At its peak the factory employed 420 wartime staff who produced over 5,300 guns during World War II. A limited amount of chocolate production continued alongside the gun manufacturing line. The factory closed 1964.

Eugenio Verrecchia emigrated to Bristol set up business in 1925. He opened the city's first ice-cream parlour, the Modern Cafe in Coronation Road, Bedminster, where Italian-style ice cream was made in huge wooden vats. The family also sold ice-cream at No.9 Peter Street which now lies under modern-day Castle Park. The factory was in Brislington, and in 1960 they launched Bristol's first ice-cream machine on wheels, with a fleet of 36 vans which toured the city seven days a week. An additional motor was fitted to supply the generating power which worked the machine and ran the freezing apparatus. Cones were filled by a tap similar to a bar pump. The family business no longer trades.

James Robertson was a leading brand of Jam and Marmalade in the UK. There was enormous demand for Golden Shred marmalade, and in 1914 a factory was opened in Brislington, Bristol. The Golliwog emblem was brought from America in 1910. The company sent out 12,000 enamel badges and 4,500 pottery golliwogs every week to children collecting the paper gollies (political correctness). In the 60s, Robertson's took over Quantock Preserving of Bridgwater and became the largest jam producer in Europe. But in 1979 the factory closed.

Plasticine was invented in Bath and made famous in Bristol. Aardman Animations was started by Peter Lord and David Sproxton in 1972 and is famous for its Claymation and stop-motion animation. Nick Park joined full time in 1985. Aardman studio has had nine Oscar® nominations, and has won four. Morph, Creature Comforts, The Wrong Trousers, Chicken Run, Shaun the Sheep and Pirates! are some of their releases.

The former offices and studios were built in the 1980s as a banana-ripening warehouse for Fyffe's. Aardman's purpose-built offices and studios, completed in 2008, are further along the road on the left. In 2005 a fire swept through a storage warehouse containing models, props and many other treasures created by the animators and designers at Aardman. The company supports the Children's Hospital and both Gromit and Shaun the Sheep sculptures have had a trail during recent summer months.

In 1960 Brooke Bond relocated from Redcliffe Backs, to a purpose built factory on Spike Island between the New Cut and Floating Harbour. Tea chests came in on the ground floor and were taken to the first floor for the unpacking and blending processes. Blended tea passed down chutes to the large assembly hall for filling bags or packets. In 1990 the factory closed, at its height producing over 1000 tea bags per minute and processing 5000 chests of tea per week.

Alfred Brooks started the company in 1862. Brooks introduced modern blanket reconditioning, shirt express, and glazing of chintz and the curling of feathers. The first motor vehicle was purchased in 1912. Brooks grew to over fifty shops and modern works at Ashley Vale when dry cleaning was introduced from France in the 1970's, This was followed closely by the hiring and processing of linen to hotels. Johnson Cleaners bought the dry cleaning company in 2003.

Bristol is HP's second-largest central research location, opened in 1983. HP Labs Bristol has developed advanced test systems for the telecoms industry; active countermeasures against computer viruses; colour systems for HP scanners; key concepts in utility and cloud computing; and software tools for the Semantic Web and context-based mobile applications. HP Labs' research is focused on five broad themes: Information Explosion, Dynamic Cloud Services, Content Transformation, Intelligent Infrastructure and Sustainability.

Wathen Gardiner, later Bristol Uniforms, began in the 1860s, providing high quality clothing. It is widely recognised as a leading designer and manufacturer of Personal Protective Equipment and specialist protective wear for the emergency services in over 110 countries. This includes firefighter clothing, bunker gear, wildland fire and rescue kit as well as technical and urban search & rescue protective clothing.

15 Financial Heritage.

Lloyds Bank, Corn St

By the early 11th century there was a mint in Bristol so it was already a place of some importance. In the 1100's, the Norman conquerors bought to Bristol Jewish financiers, who established themselves in the area just outside the walls between Broad and Small streets. By the mid-18th century, Bristol had virtually become a self-governing commercial city, ruled by her leading merchants, from among whom her mayors were chosen and economics were the determining factor.

Corn Street became a focus for the city's banks, insurance offices and coffee houses. Next to the Corn Exchange at No. 56 Corn Street was the Exchange Coffee House (pictured). Many goods were sold informally at coffee houses like this one. There were thirteen banks in Bristol by 1811. Over the next century most Bristol banks were strong enough to survive. Only two came to grief. Some main banks still have premises here but other institutions in the financial quarter of Corn Street have moved out and the buildings are now bars, restaurants and cafes.

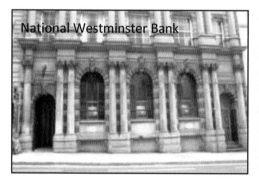
National Westminster Bank

John Vaughan was a goldsmith in the Dutch House, destroyed in the blitz. The Corporation used him for their banking needs in the early 18th century. The first true bank in Bristol, now known as the Old Bank, opened in 1750. In the late 18th century it moved opposite to what is now a pizza restaurant. This bank eventually merged into the National Westminster Bank. The plaque on the wall keeps alive the name of Bristol's first bank.

Four flat topped pillars called the Nails now stand on the pavement outside the Corn Exchange. They were relocated from along the south wall of All Saints Church. The four Nails were made at different times, and this is reflected in their varying designs. Farmers would bring samples to be sold on to merchants. These would be placed on the top of the nail and a bargain would be struck. The merchant would strike one of the Nails and place the money for the whole order on the nail and the farmer would be honour-bound to supply the goods. To pay on the nail - English phrase meaning to pay promptly.

The Corn Exchange is a Grade I listed building and the only surviving 18th century Exchange building in England. It was surrounded by coffee houses and taverns. Above and below were rooms designed as strong rooms. In the centre of the Exchange was an open court, surrounded by a colonnade. Inside the Corn Exchange the plasterwork represents the four corners of the world, including Africa and America, the latter wearing a head-dress of tobacco leaves.

This money from the trade in the slave-produced commodities from America and the Caribbean had to be administered. Loans were needed, slaving and cargo ships had to be insured. The sugar refineries and warehouses, where fire was a constant threat, required insurance as well. Goods had to be sold off and commission needed to be paid. In this way, financial services could be said to have been stimulated by the success of the triangular trade.

Commercial Rooms were built in 1810 three years after the abolition of the slave trade. The site was formerly occupied by the Foster's Coffee House another of Bristol's famous coffee houses. The exterior of the building has three statues. The statues representing Bristol, Commerce and Navigation are known as the three commercial graces. A carved relief shows Britannia checking the monies due to her. As with most of the financial institutions it is now a pub.

Bristol had its own Stock Exchange that was built in 1845. Trading was initially at Albert Chambers. Albert Fry, Chocolate, Christopher Thomas, soap, Joseph Wethered, coal and George White, aircraft, held many directorships and formed a powerfully elite. In 1903 the exchange moved to St Nicholas Street and is now a grade 2 listed building. Deals were still being made on the floor into the 1960s. With the electronic age regional exchanges came to an end and this exchange closed in 1991.

The physical growth of Bristol was made possible by the gathering of funds needed for house building. The Bristol, West of England & South Wales Permanent Building Society was founded in 1850. The building in Corn St was built in 1857 and a plaque commemorates this fact. Lloyds bank has occupied the building since the 1890's. The society shortened its name to the Bristol & West in 1935. It has since been incorporated into another financial institution.

In Broad Street is the former Bank of England branch building. It has fluted columns and unadorned capitals in the Greek Doric style. It has been designated by English Heritage as a grade I listed building. The building is now used as the Bristol Citizens Advice Bureau. Bristol is home to Head Offices in insurance, banking and the Ministry of Defence. A lot of these institutions are to be found in brand new buildings near the river by Temple Meads (pictured).

In recent years the Bristol Pound was introduced with local firms accepting this instead of pounds sterling. The Bristol Pound is the UK's first not for profit community currency and can only be used in Bristol at participating outlets. It has the backing of Bristol Credit Union. 90% of monies spent normally flows out of the city through national and international companies. It is hoped to keep this money within Bristol through recirculating, shorter supply chains and reduced carbon emissions.

16 Transport Heritage.

The Bristol Turnpike Trust was created in 1727, and grew to be one of the largest turnpike networks in England. It had powers to collect road tolls for maintenance from the 17th century. The main turnpike trust roads were the Aust Road A4018, Horfield Road A38, Stapleton Road A4058, Mangotsfield Road A432, Toghill Road A420, Bitton Road A431, Brislington Road A4, Whitchurch Road A37, Dundry Road, Winsford Road A38 and Ashton Road A370.

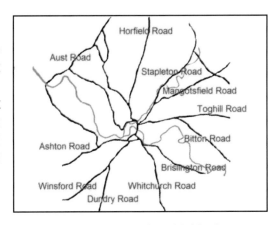

In 1802 John MacAdam moved to Bristol and in 1816 he was appointed General Surveyor of 149 miles of Bristol Roads. McAdam lived in an elegant Georgian house in Berkeley Square from 1805-1808. He is commemorated by the plaque outside where he lived. He had worked out on a new approach to road construction. He instructed that stones should be graded and laid in three levels, with the smallest stones crushed and laid as a top surface. This ensured a smoother well-drained finish.

A camber ensured rainwater rapidly drained off rather than penetrate and damage the road's foundations and were said to be 'macadamised'. The roads were dusty when it was dry and very muddy when it was wet. Gasworks tar was first used as a surface dressing, next dehydrated tar, and in 1907 tar was dehydrated and distilled to a soft pitch. Creosote was mixed with the gravel. Grade No 1 was for surface dressing and No 2 for making tarmacadam.

The Bristol Tramways Co. was founded in 1874. The horse tram depot at the junction of Perry Road and Colston Street is still visible; it is now a micro-brewery and bar. More lines opened and by 1880 there was an extensive network in the centre of the city. In 1905 the first motor bus service ran, and a bus depot and works was opened at Filton. The Good Friday raid in 1941 ended the trams by severing the power supply.

Straker-Squire opened a large factory on Lodge Causeway in 1907, and was a major producer of early London Buses, with the factory in Fishponds supplying 70% of market by 1909. Great Eastern of London took delivery of 22 in bright yellow chrome livery in 1911. The company also produced and successfully raced a number of its own car designs.

The Bristol Wagon Works, founded in 1851, moved to a 12-acre site near Lawrence Hill in 1866, where it built railway carriages and wagons, road vehicles and farm implements. Avonside Engine Works supplied the steam rail-motors power units, the firm specialised in industrial and narrow gauge tank engines. It took over part of the old Avonside Ironworks in 1882. In 1923 the Bristol Wagon Works joined with Cammell Laird Co Ltd. The premises were sold to the Bristol Tramways & Carriage Company now Lawrence Hill Bus Depot.

Bristol-built buses started in 1908. Bus manufacture moved to Brislington, the Filton works were leased to build aircraft. The trams were killed off by the blitz. The Lodekka design buses were introduced in 1953. In 1957 its name was changed to the Bristol Omnibus Company Ltd. In 1963 Bristol ended the colour bar. One-person operation started in 1968, and in 1970, the company accepted women as drivers. The Transport Act 1985 deregulated all bus services outside London. FirstGroup provided many of the same services as BT&CC.

A Bristol coach company introduced the world's first express service, linking Bristol with London. The Greyhound took eight hours from Bristol to London in in 1925. £1 return for the longest route attempted to a timetable. These coaches had solid tyres and a speed limit of 20 mph. Greyhound ran two coaches a day, leaving at 9 and 11 am. Modern coaches used to take more than six hours along the A4 before the M4 opened fully in 1971. It was absorbed by the Bristol Tramways Co. completely in 1936.

Although Isambard Kingdom Brunel was not born in Bristol, much of the work of the Victorian engineer was carried out here. He was born in 1806 in Portsmouth, Hampshire. The son of Marc Brunel, also a noted engineer, the family moved to London in 1808. When Brunel was eight he was sent to boarding school, then at fourteen he went to study in France. In late 1822, having completed his apprenticeship, Brunel returned to England. He first came to Bristol in 1828, convalescing after an accident in tunnel construction under the Thames where he almost died.

One of his many significant influences was as Engineer of the Great Western Railway. Visitors arriving by train via London are travelling on his Railway and Bristol is home to his Temple Meads Station amongst other achievements. A Gothic stone facade, built in 1840, fronted the railway terminus at Temple Meads. Five different railway lines used the station. The station was expanded in 1870's and again in the 1930's. Soon the line to London and South Wales will be electrified.

The original station now known as the Old Station, since it was superseded by later 19th century buildings, it contains the 220 ft Great Train Shed with its 72 ft single roof span, designed by Brunel. The shed was once the largest covered goods yard in Europe. This was known as the Clock Gate and was the In gateway for departures. The Out gateway for arrivals was demolished in the 1860s. There are plans for the old station to be used again when the line to London is electrified.

All the new railways which ran to or from London decided to adopt Greenwich Mean Time (GMT) right across their systems. As Bristol and London time was almost 11 minutes different, the problems were obvious. The answer, in Bristol was imaginative and the council simply added an extra minute hand to the Corn Exchange clock so it showed both Bristol and London time. The red minute hand shows railway time and the black minute hand shows Bristol time. In 1852 Bristol changed to GMT.

On open days it is possible to go behind stairs in the corn exchange and to go up onto the roof and behind the clock face to see the workings (pictured). It is wound using the handle and care has to be taken not to overwind. It is maintained twice a year by a horological engineer. The Tramway and Carriage Clock was made by William Langford, and another of his clocks can be seen at College Green, which was Bristol's first electrically regulated clock.

Brunel also created a railway system to connect Temple Meads and the docks. Brunel's scheme was to promote luxurious travel from London to North America via Bristol. The Great Western Hotel, now called Brunel House (pictured), was designed to accommodate travellers embarking on his transatlantic liner the SS Great Britain. The railway ran from Temple Meads and then parallel to Brunel's station building, crossing the road on a bridge behind the George & Railway pub and heading towards St Mary's, Redcliffe Church, through a tunnel before arriving at Prince Wharf.

Bitton Station, built from local stone, was once a thriving station, dispatching paper to London from the Golden Valley Paper Mills, soda from the Keynsham works and yellow ochre from Golden Valley. It also distributed coal and local growers sent flowers and vegetables to Bristol market. The complete closure of the Midland Railway line in 1971 meant the rapid decline of Bitton Station and the track was removed.

The Bristol Suburban Railway Society was set up in 1972 and in October 1979 the Bristol Suburban Railway Society was incorporated into the Bitton Railway Co Ltd. Many volunteers have restored the station to its former glory. Not only have the enthusiasts achieved this despite many legal and practical setbacks, they have also managed to re-lay almost three miles of track, restore several steam locomotives and many more carriages and wagons.

The Clifton Rocks Railway is a tunnelled railway between Clifton & Hotwells. The bottom entrance is on the Portway. The top entrance can be found in Sion Hill,). This water-powered 'funicular' railway opened on 11 March, 1893 and operated for 40 years, closing in 1934. It became a secret transmission base for the BBC during WWII, a repair centre for Imperial Airways barrage balloons, and a refuge shelter.

It has been empty and disused since after the war. It is brick lined in almost its entirety with a wall thickness of 2 feet. The Clifton Rocks Railway Trust has been formed to restore the Railway. Supported by the Avon Gorge Hotel, Bristol City Council and sponsored by a number of local companies the Trust is working hard to restore elements of the railway. On open doors day there is access to top station only with views down the steep tracks.

William Knee is credited with the first container shipping in 1839, when he opened a depot in Temple Street, near the station. He introduced the Knee's Furniture Van for the Removal of Furniture Without Packing. In 1844 it was the very first van to travel by train. His wheeled vehicles fitted aboard Great Western flatbed wagons to provide a roll-on, roll-off service. You loaded your Knee's van outside your own house; it travelled by road and rail and was delivered to the front door of your new home.

As the years progressed, so did the business under William Knee's sons. Knee's road'n'rail furniture vans did a roaring trade until shortly before World War I, providing the very first model for today's global container trade. After serving in the First World War Ted Knee returned to continue the removal business. After 131 years in the premises, 16 Temple Street became a target for demolition to make way for the new fire station in 1970.

In the early 20th century many cars, lorries, coaches, buses and motorcycles were produced in Bristol. Bristol Cars manufactures hand-built luxury cars. About twenty are still being built each year. Motor cycle manufacture was by Douglas Engineering of Kingswood, a firm set up in 1882 to manufacture boot making equipment. Motor cycles were first assembled in 1907, in the 1950s when it began making Vespa scooters under licence until 1964.

George Adlam & Sons Ltd, founded in the 1830's, was an iron and brass foundry and engineering company in Fishponds. It soon expanded into the former foundry of Parnall & Sons. It built machinery for the chocolate and brewing industries, and also manufactured weights, measures and shop fittings. The company also fitted out ocean liner passenger compartments on the RMS Britannic in 1929 and the famous QE2 (pictured) in the 1960s. Nearby Peckett and Sons built locomotives 1958.

Swing Bridge

There are over 40 bridges still functioning and at least six redundant ferry crossings. Many of the old ferry slipways can still be seen around the harbour. The Halfpenny, which went from Temple Back, disappeared when St Philips Bridge was built in 1841. Once the Floating Harbour was finished in 1809, the Prince Street Gibb ferry was replaced by a narrow wooden bridge. The swing bridge, divided between motorists and pedestrians, opened in 1879.

The Guinea Street ferry, took you over the water from The Grove to the Ostrich pub. Other ferries ran from Broad Quay and another from Prince's Wharf to Canons' Marsh. The Gas Works ferry took men over to work on the Great Western paddle steamer and later, on the Great Britain and at Charles Hill's shipyard. Another which plied The Cut between Coronation Road and Cumberland Road, was replaced by the present footbridge, in 1935.

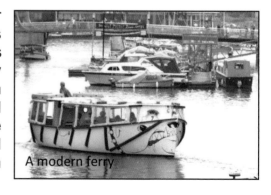

A modern ferry

The Vauxhall and the Totterdown ferries became redundant by the building of new bridges. The Mardyke Ferry running from Mardyke Wharf, Hotwells Rd to the Canada Wharf, Albion Dock started in 1854 and closed in 1962. Rownham Ferry is an ancient crossing point of the River Avon and goes back at least to the twelfth century closed in 1933 the Ferry crossed the River Avon near the entrance of the Avon Gorge. The ferry moved upstream after the expansion of Cumberland Basin in 1873.

Cross river ferry

Today services are operated both for the leisure market and for commuters to and from both the city centre and Bristol Temple Meads railway station, and serve 15 landing stages throughout the length of the harbour. Services are provided by a fleet of historic, yellow painted ferry boats. The company also runs packages which explores the impact that Brunel has had on the harbour, and the lasting effects today.

There are a few independent ferry companies which offer similar services of covered, heated ferries which run round trips to timetable all through the year. The timetable is organized by the local council. Another that provides a cross river service by the SS Great Britain. During the Green Capital year of 2015 Bristol Packet ran Hydrogenesis the UK'S first hydrogen fuel cell boat.

There are serving landing stages close to most of the harbourside attractions, which allow you to hop on and off where required. There are narrow boats and pleasure boats that offer regular harbour tours with commentaries, also river cruises up the Avon to Beeses Tea Gardens, Conham, Hanham and Bath and downstream through the gorge to Avonmouth, tides permitting.

17 Aviation Heritage.

Modern Bristol is the hot air ballooning capital of the world. In the 1780's the first hot air balloon to be seen in Britain soared over Bristol's skies and landed in St George. The first unmanned hot air balloon came to rest after its historic flight from Bath, flying west along the Avon valley to take its place in British aviation history. It landed and the event caused such a sensation that locals named the landing site Air Balloon Hill, with the local pub named after the event.

In September 1979, a small gathering of balloonists celebrated the first ever Bristol International Balloon Fiesta, when 27 balloon took part in a mass ascent. It has grown into one of the largest outdoor events in the country. It is held in Ashton Court Estate at the beginning of August. The spectacular Night Glow is where tethered balloons light up to music and the mass Balloon ascent where over 120 balloons launch across Bristol.

The Bristol Boxkite, officially the Bristol Biplane, hangs from the ceiling of the Bristol City Museum in Queen's Road, Clifton, is a contraption of strings and wire, and one of the most significant engineering products ever made. It was the brainchild of Sir George White, Bristol's tramways boss and the founder of the British and Colonial Aeroplane Company and the British aviation industry. A small 'flying ground' was built in 1911, at the top of Filton Hill.

The Boxkite was unveiled with a public flying display on Durdham Down in 1910. The plane was so successful that before long, two were being made a week and the order book was full. A Bristol Boxkite was fitted with a morse key and carried out aerial reconnaissance during manoeuvres on Salisbury Plain. It was the first time any aircraft had been flown for military purposes. A new age had begun.

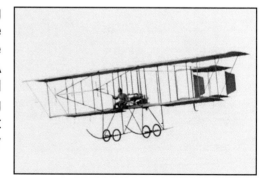

In 1929 the Council bought 298 acres in Whitchurch for the country's third municipal airport. It was requisitioned during WW2 and VIP's arrived in secrecy. The runway was last used in 1993 for an emergency landing. The old Bristol airport logo constructed in chalk still exists today although now damaged by the runway and a path. In 1955 the City Council bought Lulsgate and services were transferred there in 1957.

Old Hangers now Action Sports

Brazil Straker started an aeronautical industry in 1914 building Rolls Royce engines for the RFC in World War I. Cosmos Engineering bought the firm and designed and produced the Mercury engine before it was subsequently taken over by the Bristol Aeroplane Company in 1920. Parnall & Sons moved onto the site. From 1941 it produced aircraft components for a range of RAF aircraft including wings for De Havilland Tiger Moths and fuselages for Short Stirling bombers. Post war, Parnall & Sons continued manufacturing aircraft interiors and fuselages until about 1960. Today, Diamonite Aircraft Furnishings supplies top end aircraft interiors.

The latest in that line is the giant Airbus A380. Before she has made her first flight, this aircraft has redefined air travel, in the numbers of people she will carry, the facilities aboard and in her sheer size. She may not have the originality of the Box Kite, the propeller-driven grace of the mighty Brabazon or the revolutionary look of Concorde, but the name of Bristol and the 1,000 people who work on the wings, landing gear and fuel systems at Filton will be written into another chapter of aviation history.

British Aerospace, a major aerospace and engineering group, and one of the world's leading defence and aerospace companies built its Sowerby Research Centre in Filton in 1982. Aircraft are designed and constructed here, including the Anglo-French Concorde supersonic airliner. British Aerospace was responsible for the first plane capable of flying nonstop across the Atlantic, the Vickers Vimy.

The other firsts include the Viscount, the world's first turbo-prop airliner service first flown in 1948; Concorde, the first and only operational Supersonic Transport in service from 1976 to 2003; the Vulcan, the first delta wing jet bomber from 1956 until 1984; the Harrier, the first Vertical/Short Take Off and Landing (V/STOL) fighter; entered service in the mid-1980s, and finally, the Seawolf, the first anti-missile missile to defeat a 4.5 inch shell.

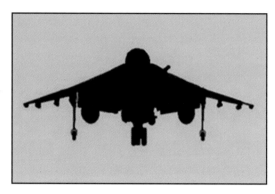

Bristol has had a hand in creating an aircraft that sets new standards. Many of the engines including the Olympus 593, are designed and built by Rolls Royce in Filton. Concorde's maiden flight took off from Filton. Eurofighter is intended to meet Europe's air defence needs into the 21st century. The old industrial museum had a superb collection of aero engines and there are models of most of the famous aircraft made here, including the Blenheim, Britannia and Brabazon.

18 Cultural Heritage.

Bristol city centre is the commercial, cultural and business centre of the City. The course of the River Frome was covered over in stages during the second half of the 19th century. The area became known as the Tramways Centre even after the last trams left in 1941, but is now known simply as the Centre. The City Centre was also redeveloped leading up to the millennium. The flower gardens were removed and replaced by three large water fountains.

The hop on / hop off sightseeing bus allows access to most of the attractions further away from the Harbourside. The commentaries are spoken by guides. Questions can be asked along the journey. A round trip takes 1 hour 15 minutes, with at least 20 different stops taking in Brunel's SS Great Britain, the Avon Gorge, the Clifton Suspension Bridge the Bristol Zoo, Temple Meads, Cabot Circus, Clifton Village, Park Street; and St. Nicholas Market

The oldest theatre in Bristol was located in Jacob Wells Road. It closed in 1779. The Theatre Royal in King Street, built in the seventeenth century as the New Theatre, is Britain's oldest continually worked theatre. It was set up by 50 wealthy local business men, many of whom were Merchant Venturers and they all invested £50 in the building. The first performance was in 1766 the year it gained its Royal status.

The Theatre is grade I listed building. It incorporates the eighteenth-century Coopers' Hall, built in 1744, as its foyer. Coopers' Hall is a grade II listed building. At its height the theatre could house 1680 people catering to three distinct types of clientele, the pit, the gallery and the boxes. After WW2 the Arts Council asked the Old Vic to start the provincial company, the Bristol Old Vic. A £12million extension / refurbishment was completed in 2012 as pictured.

King Street was laid out in 1650 to develop the Marsh outside the city walls. It once led down to the docks at Welsh Back, where the old sailing trows used to dock after their journeys from South Wales. The Llandroger Trow pub dates back to 1663. It is rumoured to have been patronised by Robert Louis Stevenson whilst writing Treasure Island after hearing Alexander Selkirk's story. In 1775 both Henry Webb, captain of the slaver, the Nevis Planter, and Robert Walls, surgeon on the Guinea slaver, lived there. Many of the houses are of historical interest.

The north side of King Street was developed first in 1650 and the south side in 1663, and was named after Charles II. The street is home to many grade II* buildings. Many original features can be seen, including timber frames and oriel windows. Built in 1653, numbers 33-34 are the only surviving buildings of the original development. There is still a section of the old town wall hidden away. Number 35 is a former cork warehouse. Number 7 and 8 make use of recycled ships timbers.

The Old Library was founded in 1613, and was the third public library in the country. It was originally housed in the King Street lodge of Bristol merchant Robert Redwood, who donated it to Bristol Corporation. In 1772 it was a subscription Library. The city made it free to the public from 1856. In 1876 after a refurbishment it was renamed as the Central Library. In 1906 the library was moved to the newly built Bristol Central Library. The King Street building eventually became a restaurant. It has been designated by English Heritage as a grade II* listed building (pictured).

Bristol Byzantine is a type of architecture built from 1850 to 1880. The style is characterised by colours including red, yellow, black and white brick primarily from the Cattybrook Brickpit. The first building with some of the characteristics generally thought of a Bristol Byzantine is Bush House, built in grey stone. The Granary (pictured) on Welsh Back was built in 1869 with red brick with black and white brick and limestone dressings. It is the best preserved example of the Bristol Byzantine style. It has been a granary, a nightclub, a jazz club now it has been renovated and converted into apartments. a grade II* listed building.

Others include the Wool Hall which housed the city's wool market. The building is now a live music venue named The Fleece. Other examples include the premises of Hardware (Bristol) Limited in Old Bread Street, the St Vincent's Works in Silverthorne Lane, Robinson's Warehouse on Bathurst Parade, the Gardiners warehouse in Broad Plain, the Carriage Works in Stokes Croft, the former cork warehouse in King Street and Brown's Restaurant in Queens Street.

Old Market originally was the area directly outside the castle where the troops mustered. An autumn fair was held here and market days always attracted suspicious characters and petty crimes, but detaining suspects for a later trial over trivial offences was a costly nuisance. The Pie Poudre Court was established to sort out disputes and punish misdemeanours on the spot. Pie Poudre comes from the Norman which means Pie (pied, or foot) and Poudre (powder) and together they form an expression meaning 'dusty feet' or raga-muffins. These proclamations took place outside the Stag and Hounds. The sign still hangs declaring Pie Poudre Court, Established 1483.

The Red Lodge was built in 1580. The plain red door and the red stone exterior conceal hidden treasures. The house and grounds of the Carmelite Friary, were bought by Bristol Corporation in 1538and later sold to Sir John Younge who built his Great House on the site of the present Colston Hall circa 1570. He added the White Lodge, to the east, and the Red Lodge, up the hill. The house was altered around 1730, and restored in the early 20th century. It is a grade I listed building.

James Cowles Prichard wrote The Natural History of Man while living at The Red Lodge from 1827. It was the country's first girls' reform school set up in 1854 by Mary Carpenter, one of the originators of the Reformatory system for poor girls and a pioneer of philanthropic work. It was set up with the financial help of the poet Lord Byron's widow, who bought the Red Lodge in 1854. The reformatory school eventually closed in 1917.

Benefactors bought, renovated and presented the Red Lodge to the City of Bristol. The city leased it to the Bristol Savages, a society of artists whose history dates back to the late Victorian era. Native American culture still plays a large part in its traditions. Since 1948, the Red Lodge and its garden has been in the care of the City of Bristol Museum and Art Gallery

The Tudor period is shown by the Great and Small Oak rooms and a bedroom. The print room, parlour and reception room are from the Georgian era, and the Exhibition Room contains a display on the Red Lodge Girls Reform School. The south-facing, walled garden is a re-created Elizabethan-style knot garden with herbaceous borders. The box hedge design is a replica of the pattern from the lodge's bedroom ceiling. All the plants grown here could have been found in English gardens by 1630.

Bristol's first telephone exchange catered for 25 subscribers, opened in 1879. Sharing offices with the Victoria Tea Company, it was housed on the corner of Mary-Le-Port Street, in the Queen Victoria building, demolished in 1960. There is a commemorative plaque on the building which replaced it. Butler's tar works was the first local firm to use the service, between their works and their head office in St Philips. By 1886, Bristol had freestanding call offices where a three-minute call could be made for just 2d.

In 1900 a move was made to Telephone Avenue where it would remain until 1992. In 1958 the Queen made the first-ever directly dialled long-distance phone call in the UK from there marking the inauguration of Subscriber Trunk Dialling, or STD. It also meant that pay on answer phones began to supersede the Press button A and B models. In 1983, Princess Anne arrived in Bristol to inaugurate a revolutionary new phone system which incorporated both pictures and sound.

Bristol City Museum and Art Gallery is situated next to the Wills University building, housing regional, national and international exhibits. The building is of Edwardian Baroque architecture and has been designated by English Heritage as a grade II* listed building. Its origins begin in 1823. In 1871 the Bristol Institution merged with the Bristol Library Society and in 1872 the combined museum and library building was opened. It was transferred to Bristol Corporation in 1894. The Art Gallery was added in 1905.

The harbourside is home to a myriad of museums. There is the internationally renowned SS Great Britain and Maritime Heritage Centre. The M Shed depicts the life and times of Bristol and Bristolians. Docked outside the M Shed are the boats the Mayflower, the Pyronaut and the John King tug (pictured). The Fairbairn steam crane was finished in 1878. It was built to handle heavy lifts up to 35 tons. It is a working Scheduled Ancient Monument.

There was a real danger of a fire that started aboard one ship spreading to all of the others, with no chance of controlling the spread. Crowded docks surrounded by warehouses can be disastrous and waterborne fire-engines can fight the fire from the water. All firefighting in Bristol was carried out either by private insurance companies or the Docks Company until the formation of the Bristol Fire Brigade as a branch of the police in 1876.

In 1934 the Bristol Phoenix II (later Pyronaut) was launched. In 1940 Pyronaut embarked upon her busiest period, as the air raids of the Bristol Blitz damaged and destroyed countless warehouses, factories, shops and homes around the Floating Harbour. By 1967 she was obsolete. Bristol City Museum and Art Gallery began restoration and preservation in 1995. Listed as part of the National Historic Fleet Collection, she performs displays during major harbour events.

The Müller Museum in Cotham Park reflects on the life and work of George Müller, founder of the Müller Homes for Children, and has been recently refurbished and is housed in a fine Italianate style Victorian Villa. The Concrete House is a classic 'Modern Movement' house built in 1934 and still with many of its original fixtures and fittings.

Glenside Hospital Museum of the Mind displays life in this Psychiatric Hospital from 1861 to 1994. The Bristol Lunatic Asylum became the First World War Beaufort War Hospital and then the Glenside Psychiatric Hospital. When the Hospital closed in 1994, the use of the derelict chapel was given to the Museum. The museum has a wide range of artefacts and images from the life of Glenside and of the local Learning Disability Hospitals of the Stoke Park Group and the Burden Neurological Institution.

Elsie Briggs House of Prayer in Westbury on Trym was built in 1445 and is one of the oldest lived in buildings in Bristol. Its many original features include 15th century windows, oak front door and roof timbers, which show fine examples of medieval building methods. It and the cottage next door is Grade 2* listed. Dr Briggs lived here from 1958 and uncovered its 15th century features. In 1988, she left it to the Diocese of Bristol as an ecumenical House for contemplative prayer.

Other houses situated around Bristol include the Merchants' Hall, Clifton, which is the home of Bristol's Merchant Venturers, an important influence on Bristol's history for more than 450 years. It contains fine paintings and historic artefacts in an imposing Victorian mansion. The Mansion House is a splendid Italianate official residence of the Lord Mayor since 1874. The building can be available for wedding ceremonies. Only Bristol, York and London have a Mansion House.

Merchants Hall

The Wills Memorial Building was one of the last Gothic buildings constructed in England and was designed in 1912 by Sir George Oatley. It was commissioned and funded by Sir George A Wills and Mr. Henry Herbert Wills, the tobacco magnates, in honour of their father, Henry Overton Wills, benefactor and first Chancellor of the University. The Wills family has donated millions of pounds to the University. The Octagonal Lantern contains England's sixth largest bell, Great George, a deep E-flat bell.

University College opened in 1876 offering courses in 15 subjects. It grew over the following twenty five years with the Bristol Medical School incorporated into the College. The Colston Society began to support the college and the push to become a university began. After the first donation by H O Wills, and the merger between Merchant Venturers College and the University College, the University of Bristol was given its Royal Charter

Millennium square and Anchor Square were developed in 2000 as part of the largest inner-city urban regeneration project in Europe and contains shops, cafes, sculptures and artwork. Transit sheds and goods yards once occupied the area. @Bristol is a world-class learning and leisure experience and hands-on science centre, housed in the Great Western Railway goods shed, one of the earliest surviving reinforced concrete buildings in the UK.

The silver sphere accommodates the immersive Planetarium featuring 360° digital 3D, 4K Ultra High Definition and incredible 7.1 surround sound. Several pieces of public art enhance the square with statues of Bristol legends and water sculptures. The water sculptures, water pools and light features present hours of enjoyment for youngsters. The square provides a focal point during festivals and events. Large screens show major televised events.

Bristol Hippodrome has seating on three levels giving a capacity of 1951. The theatre was opened on 16 December 1912. It has a dome, which can be opened, however since air conditioning it is rarely opened. The theatre survived World War 2 but three years after, a fire destroyed the stage but did not reach the auditorium which was saved. Its stage is one of the largest outside of London and features West End Shows when they tour, the yearly traditional pantomime, Welsh National Opera, the Bristol Gang Show and 'one night shows'.

The Nonesuch is the City's floral emblem. From mediaeval times, the Nonesuch or Scarlet Lychnis was known as the Flower of Bristowe. It was brought to Europe from the Middle East by the returning Crusaders. The brilliant scarlet colour was later chosen for the University's academic hoods. The university's first boat, almost over 100 years ago was called Nonesuch. The Nonesuch is the biannual magazine for the University. Today the flower grows wild in some parts of the Avon River Gorge.

Queen Victoria granted Bristol a Lord Mayor in 1899. The Lord Mayor robes, hat, jabot and gauntlets have their origins in medieval times. Scarlet is a royal colour and was worn as early as 1415. The more fur on the robe, the greater the authority. The hat is a black-feathered tricorn. Bristol has four swords for civic use. The Lord Mayor sometime wears Velvets and a dress sword. Today only the Lord Mayors of London and Bristol are entitled to wear them. Bristol is the only city outside London to have a State Coach.

This stone is set into the base of the wall enclosing Cotham Parish Church. Bewell's Cross, also called Gallows Cross stood in the Gallows Field at the top of St Michael's Hill, the road to Wales. The cross also served as a boundary marker of the County of Bristol. Bewell's Cross was one of many in the Bristol area, such as the High Cross in the High Street; St Peter's Cross near St Peter's church; the Stallage Cross in Temple Street; and Don John's Cross at St George.

The curved section of stone wall on the corner and the gateway a little further along Cumberland Road are the last remains of Bristol's New Gaol. Built in 1816, it suffered considerable damage during the Bristol Riots of 1831. The cells were 6 foot by 9 foot and held 197 prisoners. It continued in use until 1883, with regular public executions on top of the gateway until 1845. The last execution was of a servant girl, Sarah Harriet Thomas, in 1849. The remains of the gaol, have been designated by English Heritage as a grade II listed building.

New Gaol

Christmas Steps was originally a steep, muddy and narrow street. The River Frome came almost to the end of the hill. The street led up from the Frome Bridge, outside the city walls and was the start of the road to the Aust Ferry and thereon to Wales. This is an old part of Bristol, with several buildings a couple of hundred years old. The fish and chip shop at the bottom is around 300 years old. Christmas Steps was home to cutlers, makers of blade-edged steel weapons and tools, and armourers. A stone plaque states how the street was 'steppered done and finished in September 1669' the cobbled slopes and steps remain today and contain specialist traders.

Erected in 1375 to commemorate the granting of a charter by Edward III, making Bristol the first provincial borough to be a county in its own right, it stood at the junction of Broad Street, Cork Street, High Street and Wine Street. The height was increased in 1633. In 1733 there was a petition for its removal and it was then re-erected in College Green, but was taken down in 1762 after two years it was given to Henry Hoare, who reassembled the cross at Stourhead. The statues of four monarchs are displayed in alcoves in the second tier of the cross, with four more seated in the third. King John and Charles I faced north along Broad Street, Henry III and Henry VI faced east along Wine Street, Edward IV and James I faced south along High Street and Edward III and Elizabeth I faced west along Corn Street.

19 Social and Medical Heritage.

Apart from a City of Churches Bristol has been called a City of Charities. By 1230, six hospitals had been founded on the outskirts of the city where the poor could find shelter and food. These hospitals were the forerunner of alms-houses. The earliest alms-house was founded in 1292 in Long Row, between St Thomas Street and Temple Street. The building was destroyed in the Blitz. Bristol Charities came into being as a result of the 1835 Municipal Corporations Act.

The oldest charity was founded in 1395, and the most recent was formed in 2003.The Holy Trinity Hospital, also known as Barstaple Alms-houses, was founded in 1395 by the merchant John Barstaple and is situated at the corner of Old Market Street and Midland Road. It has been rebuilt and the present building dates back to mid-Victorian times. Since 1836, it is owned and managed by the Trustees of Bristol Charities and provides accommodation for 30 residents.

Foster, who made his money trading in cod and salt was rich enough to be able fund the building of the 15th century alms-houses and chapel at the top of Christmas Steps which is a Grade II listed building. The alms-house has been rebuilt twice, first in 1708 and again in 1883. A new alms-house, but still bearing the John Foster name, was recently opened in Crow Lane, Henbury by the Princess Royal.

Colton's Alms-houses is on St Michaels Hill. The alms-houses were founded by Edward Colston for 24 inmates, the 12 men and 12 women residents had to be Bristol-born and attend the chapel regularly. It was built in 1691 and has been designated by English Heritage as a grade I listed building. The front wall and gates are also grade I listed. The clock, belfry and barrel-vaulted chapel, panelled with ships' timbers, has had with few alterations since it was built.

St Nicholas' Alms-houses is a building on King Street. It was built in 1652 to 1656, extended in the 19th century and restored 1961. The foundations of a bastion of the City Wall were revealed during restoration, and is designated by English Heritage as a grade II* listed building. The alms-house was one of the first buildings in King Street, a new development then outside the city wall and beside the "Back Street Gate". The building was damaged during the Bristol Blitz and now presents only a facade to the street.

Other buildings that are no longer alms-houses are Bengough's in Horfield Road, which were built in 1818. The alms-houses became a care home in 1996 and were later converted into flats. Stevens Alms-houses in Old Market Street was built in 1679 and was pulled down in the war restoration of 1957. Merchant Taylors' Alms-houses in Merchant Street, is now a bank, was founded in 1701. Above the door is a large, painted panel bearing the arms of the Merchant Taylor's Guild.

Bristol Royal Infirmary was founded in 1735 and received its royal title from Queen Victoria in 1850. Voluntary hospitals were independent and relied on private sources of funding. In 1904, Sir George White, saved the hospital from a major financial crisis and later helped to construct the Edward VII Memorial Wing in 1912. The National Health Service began in 1948. The facilities were greatly extended in the 1960s. The Queen's building was opened in 1973.

The old building opened in 1737 and closed when new wards were built next to the Queen's building in 2015. The building at one time housed a number of wards that were among the oldest clinical environments in use in the country. The Infirmary was founded with the pledges of 78 Bristol citizens who each gave between two and six guineas 'to benefit the poor sick'. Somehow it is not a listed building.

In 1865 a home for the rescue of young girls who have gone astray was founded providing education, training and support. The home was the Bristol Female Mission Society, run and funded by women for women. Bristol Maternity Hospital was opened on the site in 1914. In 1950, the hospital, moved to Redland. In 1972 maternity services relocated to the current St Michael's building. In 2003, a birthing suite and the Lavender bereavement suite opened.

Bristol Homeopathic Hospital can be traced back to premises on the Triangle in 1852. A new hospital was commissioned in 1921 and continued to provide a full range of services until 1986. A purpose-built hospital opened in 1994. The Bristol Haematology & Oncology Centre is situated on Cotham Hill. The Oncology Centre opened in 1971 and Haematology Services were centralised at the centre in the 1990s. In 2013, the Bristol Homeopathic Hospital moved to South Bristol Community Hospital.

Bristol Royal Hospital for Sick Children inpatient department was founded in 1866 by Liberal politician Mark Whitwell. An outpatients department had been in use since 1857 in Royal Fort Road. The St Michaels Hill site was opened in 1885 and became 'Royal' in 1897. Wallace & Gromit's Grand Appeal raised over £12m towards the new site which opened in 2001. It was a purpose-built children's hospital and brings all children's services under one roof.

University of Bristol Dental Hospital and the Dental School exist together. They lie on the site of the earliest known Romano- British settlement, then of the religious establishment of Franciscans Friars or Greyfriars built around 1250. Dental surgeons have been trained here since 1906 and complementary dentistry since 1972. An expansion was completed in 2009 which enabled the number of dental undergraduates to be increased to 75 per year.

The Institution for the Cure of Disease of the Eye Amongst the Poor was founded in 1808. In 1839 and 1898 the Bristol Eye Hospital continued to grow. Another new building was completed in 1935 and this in turn was demolished in 1982 to make way for the present hospital. The hospital developed Retinal Services, the Clinical Research Unit and developed a paediatric outpatients department and was completed in 2011.

The Bristol General Hospital originally opened in 1832 taking only patients from the Bristol area, and expanding to outside Bristol in 1850. Two new wings were added before the First World War to provide medical and maternity wards and a dental department. The radiotherapy department was based here until the advent of cobalt radiation treatment in the early 1960s highlighted the need for a purpose built centre. It closed in 2012 and care transferred to the South Bristol Community Hospital.

The School of Anatomy and Medicine and the Bristol Medical and Surgical School merged together in 1832. In 1876 The Medical School was affiliated to the new University College of Bristol. In 1899 the students used both the Infirmary and the General for clinical studies. During WW1 many other buildings were requisitioned for hospital use, including Kingsweston, Bruce Cole Institute, Ashton Court Hospital and Beaufort War Hospital.

In the 1920's there was a proposal to unite all the Bristol hospitals but it was not for another 20 years until the General and the Bristol Royal Infirmary joined forced. From 1947 to 1974 NHS services were managed by the South-Western Regional Hospital Board, then by Avon Area Health, which divided services into three areas, Bristol and Weston, Southmead and Frenchay. In 1991 United Bristol Healthcare NHS Trust and the North Bristol NHS Trust were formed.

In 2008 the Trust achieved Foundation Trust status and became the University Hospitals Bristol NHS Foundation Trust. The University Hospitals Bristol NHS Foundation Trust runs Bristol Royal Infirmary and Bristol Royal Hospital for Children, Bristol Eye Hospital, South Bristol Community Hospital, Bristol Haematology and Oncology Centre, St Michael's Hospital, Heart Institute Clinical Services, Homeopathic Hospital and the University of Bristol Dental Hospital.

In 1907 Cossham Memorial Hospital opened from funds bequeathed by Handel Cossham, He was the owner of Kingswood Colliery and represented East Bristol in Parliament. The hospital was built for the working people of East Bristol and South Gloucestershire, who were largely miner's families. The clock tower is the highest point in Bristol and can be seen for miles around, it is designated by English Heritage as a grade II listed building.

A municipal sanatorium at Frenchay Park was used to treat tuberculous children. During 1938-1940 the Hospital was constructed and the American Army used it as an Evacuation Hospital. Several medical establishments in the city were destroyed, including St Peters Hospital, during the blitz. In the years after the war Thoracic and Neurosurgery Units and a Plastic Surgery Unit were established at Frenchay Hospital. In 1961 a Burns Unit was set up and in 1974 Bristol first EMI (CT) scanner is installed.

Southmead hospital first opened as a 64 bed workhouse for poor sick people in 1902. It was then used as an army hospital during WW1 before again becoming a workhouse. In the mid 1929 Southmead Infirmary was built as a municipal institution for 'all necessitous sick persons'. A Maternity wing was added. TB cases were moved to Ham Green, mentally Ill to Stapleton and the aged to Eastville. After WW2 the hospital expanded to how it is today.

In the 21st century Frenchay, Southmead, Cossham and Clevedon hospitals, and the unit at Yate West Gate Centre formed the North Bristol NHS trust. Also incorporated was the Bristol Centre for Enablement (pictured), the Riverside Unit and the Young People's Community. These units deal with Mobility, Prosthetics and Orthotics, an Eating Disorder programme and Service and education for North Bristol and South Gloucester.

In March 2014 the new £430m hospital was completed. The major trauma centre, accident and emergency, plastics and adult burns, neurosciences units moved from Frenchay Hospital to Southmead. Specialist children's services moved from Frenchay to the Bristol Children's Hospital, whilst other services moved to the new building. The new Brunel building, named after the famous engineer, brings all the service under one roof and is designed for the 21st century

In 1977, Steptoe and Edwards carried out a pioneering conception which resulted in the birth of the world's first baby to be conceived by IVF. Lesley Brown's blocked fallopian tubes meant getting pregnant naturally was impossible for her and her husband. Lesley signed up to the experimental procedure and it worked the first time. She made medical history on July 25th, 1978, when she gave birth to daughter Louise. Edwards was awarded the 2010 Nobel Prize in Physiology or Medicine.

The Stapleton Lunatic Asylum opened in 1857. During World War I it became Beaufort Military Hospital and later known as Glenside Psychiatric Hospital. Several Grade II listed buildings are on the site, including the top and lower lodge, the main hospital, the former isolation block and the former chapel. In 1831 the old French Prisoner of war camp was taken over. It was a work-house from 1837 In 1865 it was rebuilt and has become Manor Park Hospital since 1946.

Manor Park Hospital

Beech House

Purdown was part of the manor of Barton Regis. Heath House was bought by Robert Thorne, it passed to a branch of the Smyth family in 1767. The medieval house was demolished in 1783-4 and a new building was erected. The house was bought privately by the Reverend Harold Burden in 1911. Along with Beech House and the Tower it became Purdown Hospital, an extension of Stoke Park Colony for the "amelioration of young people of enfeebled mind". Heath House is now Priory hospital.

Stoke Park Colony, founded in 1909, was the first institution certified as a home for mentally retarded patients. The colony was built in the grounds owned by the Duke of Beaufort. The hospital closed in 1997. In the grounds is an obelisk, built in 1762 It is a moulded pedestal but the top is missing. There was once a Latin inscription to the Duke of Beaufort's niece, whose death it commemorates.

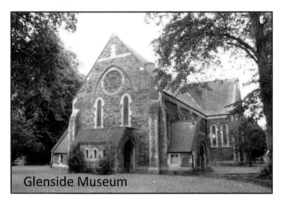
Glenside Museum

The Burden Neurological Institute opened in 1939 at Stoke Park Hospital and lasted on the site until 2000. The Institute continued to operate at Frenchay Hospital until 2015, it then moved to the new hospital at Southmead. The site of the former chapel at Glenside now houses the Glenside Museum. The museum has images from Glenside and of the local Learning Disability Hospitals of the Stoke Park Group and the Burden Neurological Institution.

There is no evidence of the large workhouse that once stood at 100 Fishponds Road, apart from the boundary wall and entrance pillars which still show 100. Originally it was under the control of the Clifton Poor Law Union, renamed Barton Regis, and was built in 1847. In 1930 it became a home for the aged. It was finally demolished in 1972 and was replaced by the Maytrees Home for the Blind. This has now also gone, and was replaced by modern housing.

Hillfields was bought from the Duke of Beaufort in the early 20th Century to become the first council housing estate to be built in Bristol. These homes for hero's returning from WW1 were started in 1919 and paved the way for the welfare state. The houses and gardens on the estate were generous; the estate was further developed in 1922 to meet the demands of the new industries that were growing up in the area. The plaque can be seen between 84 and 86 Beechen Drive.

In 1898 and 1904 the city was extended to take in some suburbs. Between 1919 and 1939, new estates were built at Southmead, Knowle, Filwood Park, Sea Mills and Horfield and the boundaries were again extended to encompass these districts. After WW2 the first prefabs were completed in June 1945. Pre-cast Reinforced Concrete houses were built during the 1950s and 1960s, with the development of peripheral estates on the edge of the city, including Withywood, Lockleaze, and Lawrence Weston.

Lockleaze Council Houses

20 Utilities.

The production of tar led to the introduction of coal-gas lighting. Gas lighting companies were formed in many large towns and cities and the practice of carbonising coal developed rapidly. In Bristol, in contrast to most large cities, the supply of gas, water and urban transport services was the province of private firms, although attempts were made at intervals to take over the operations of the Tramways Co.

In medieval times, monks and friars supplied water from local springs through wooden and lead piping. St. Mary Redcliffe's water supply came from a spring in Knowle. The Jacobs Wells pipe supplied water to Bristol Cathedral and the St. Johns conduit spring came from the north east of Brandon Hill. Quay Pipe belonged to the City and came from two springs coming down from Ashley hill. An old custom to preserve the rights of the spring was called "walking the pipe".

Prior to 1847 the city relied on piped spring water, river water, spa water, wells and rainwater. Wells were built over some of the many springs, such as St Edith's Well in Castle Park, Mother Pugsley's Well in Kingsdown and Bewell's Well. It was said that the local beer was safer to drink than the water. Once the city had an adequate supply of clean water, public health improved dramatically and rid Bristol of its reputation as the third unhealthiest city in the country.

For their religious customs the Jewish financiers needed two sources of water, one for the washing of their dead and the other for purification rituals. There is a possible ritual bath in Jacobs Wells Road. The community adopted the Jacob's Well spring and it is likely that the Garden Spring on the opposite side of the path would be used by travellers. The expulsion of the Jews in 1290 meant the spring water once more ran free down to the river Avon.

A hot spring issues from rocks below St. Vincent Cliffs above the Avon Gorge. In 1695 a Pump Room and lodging house was built to drink the waters, it became known as The Hotwells. All that's left of this Spa is the Colonnade, on the Portway, and is an 18th-century Grade II* listed terrace. The terrace was erected as a row of shops for visitors to The Hot Wells. There are spear headed railings and gates to the flagged pavement and to the front garden. They fall within the Clifton conservation area.

In 1841, the Merchant Venturers built a Pumping House using springs for the benefit of Clifton. Leders carried water to homes and would charge a penny a pail. The Sion Spring was discovered in the 1780s. Sion Spring House shows where the spring once emerged, there were other springs at Buckingham Place, Richmond Place and Whiteladies Road. By the end of the 17th Century Bristol water was being shipped all over the world. Glass-making originated from the popularity of Bristol's spring water years ago.

Pumps were very much in use in the 16th and 17th, and even the 18th centuries. Robert Lang donated one hundred pounds in 1859 for a fountain. Alderman Proctor's fountain stands on the Downs on The Promenade near the top of Bridge Valley Road. Other fountains were privately supplied as well as by the Waterworks Company, but they have almost disappeared. The provision of piped water to Bristol houses began in the mid-19th Century, although it took a long while for the demise of the communal pump. By 1906 there were at least 40 drinking fountains in various places in Bristol.

In 1845 the Bristol Waterworks Company, formed to provide for the poorer, more densely-populated areas of Bristol by bringing in fresh water from the Mendips. William Budd was a leading advocate for cleaning up water. In 1846 the Bristol Waterworks Company was formally established by an Act of Parliament. Soon clear water travelled from Chewton Mendip through 16km of conduit, into the heart of Bristol.

The first of three Barrow Reservoirs was built in 1850. Sand filters, chlorination and micro-straining were introduced to treat the water. In 1888 a reservoir was built at Blagdon. Cheddar springs were first tapped in 1922, and a full reservoir created in the 1930s. Chew Reservoir was eventually opened in 1956. Half the water is taken from the Mendip Hills, with the other half is piped from the River Severn via the Gloucester and Sharpness Canal.

A reservoir has been formed at Clywedog in mid-Wales. Treatment works were developed, at Littleton and Purton, to treat the river water. Improvement in July 1995 included ozone disinfection and granular activated carbon filtration. There are 6,382 km of local water mains. In the driest weather, Bristol hardly ever restricts water thanks to the Rivers, Boreholes, Catchment Reservoirs, Springs and Wells.

An act of 1749 made it the responsibility of householders to pitch and pave half of the street, to light a lantern each night and to clean the street. Gas lighting was first used in Bristol in 1811. In the early 20th century iron kerbing, almost unique to Bristol, was used to prevent cartwheel damage, some can be found in King Street amongst other places. They were made by the Douglas Company of Kingswood, who used left over metal from the manufacture of their famous motorcycles.

Lamplighters pub Shirehampton

A lamplighter lit street lights, generally by means of a wick on a long pole. At dawn, they would return and turn them off using a small hook on the same pole. Early street lights were candles, oil, and similar consumable liquid or solid lighting sources with wicks. Lamplighters also renewed the candles, oil, or gas mantles. In the 19th century, gas lights became the form of street lighting. Early gaslights required lamplighters, but systems were developed which allowed the lights to operate automatically.

In 1817, John Breillat set up the Bristol Gas Lighting Company. By 1820 this company was lighting most of the main streets with coal gas. Before this time, lighting was by whale oil lamps and candles. In 1853 the rival companies in Bristol amalgamated to form The United Gas Light Co. In 1878 they bought 40 acres in Stapleton Road in Eastville to become the city's main gas-producing site. In 1891, the company became Bristol Gas Company. By the turn of last century, they were responsible for lighting nearly 9,000 street lamps. Suggs and Company of London made these in the early nineteenth century. The company still exists and is today making the reproduction models. There are still 21 working gas-lamps in Bristol.

Stokers had to load the furnaces by hand and then rake out the coke. The heat was intense as gas is produced by heating coal to a temperature of some 2000° F. Many stokers succumbed to cancers of the lung and bladder amongst others. 1450 tons of coal was being used each day to produce the gas. By 1905 machines allowed the vast amounts of coal needed to be fed into them by gravity and the coke released below.

The gas was condensed, distilled and cleaned. The clean gas was held in a Gasometer. During the First World War 30 to 40 women were employed as stokers. By 1930 there were more than 100,000 customers throughout the city. Pre-paid meters were installed in homes in 1890 and proved very popular. By 1914, half of all the company's 65,000 customers were using meters.

In 1949 the gas industry was nationalised and in 1957 there was a major new installation at the Stapleton Road site, where production was concentrated. In the 1960s, coal gas production was phased out and production moved to oil-gas works at Avonmouth. When natural gas arrived in 1975, it was the end of production. The derelict oil and gas buildings at Harbourside are being transformed into offices, homes and shops.

The old home of Bristol Rovers FC was close to the Stapleton Road site. The nearby Gasometers could be seen between the Tote End and the North Stand. The smell permeated the ground and the fans began to be called "the gas" or "gasheads".

Electricity, the last of the great nineteenth-century public utilities, was from the outset in the hands of the local authority. In 1893 the street lighting system in Bristol used carbon arc lights connected to a D.C. system in series 50 yards apart. The lamps were connected by single core cables starting and finishing at Temple Back Electricity Works. If one lamp failed, then the whole circuit failed. In 1899, with ever increasing demand, a large new site of 9.5 acres at St. Philip's Marsh was purchased.

21 Parks, Gardens and Open Spaces.

Bristol has proportionately more parks and green spaces than any other UK city. So you're never far from a great place to relax, picnic or watch the world go by. Some of Bristol's highlights are its heritage estates, such as Ashton Court, Arnos Vale and Blaise Castle. As well as Castle Park, College Green, Queens Square, the Downs and the thickly wooded slopes of the Avon gorge. Most Victorian suburbs have their own park.

The Downs, Clifton and Durdham Downs, make up more than 400 acres of grassland stretching from the very cliffs of the Avon Gorge to the edges of the Victorian-built suburbs. In 1861, the Society of Merchant Venturers gave Clifton Down to the public forever, while Durdham Down was purchased from the Lords of the Manor of Henbury. Originally the Downs were rough pasture land used for sheep grazing. There were also lead-mines and stone-quarries.

In the 19th century horse-races were held, especially at Easter, as well as wrestling and boxing contests and cricket matches. The Clifton slide is a marble-like track of limestone rubbed smooth by generations of children's trousers and skirts on the rock just below the Observatory. The Downs Football League is a stand alone league formed in 1905 and does not feed into the league pyramid. All matches are played on one site, with fifty teams playing in four divisions.

Bristol's International Festival of Kites & Air Creations used to take Ashton Court by storm. The Festival features spectacular flying displays, and breath-taking choreographed routines as well as colourful examples of kites, banners and inflatable of all shapes and sizes. Recently the festival has taken place on Durham Downs. The festival started in 1986 with a working budget of only £300 and now, it is an annual festival.

The Observatory, St Vincent's Cave and Camera Obscura are close to the Suspension Bridge. Originally a snuff mill it was partially destroyed during a strong gale in 1777 The Observatory is situated high on a hill 338 feet above the river. St Vincent's Cave (the Giant's Cave) is just below the tower. An underground path cuts through the rock ending at a platform half way down the gorge. It is some 250 feet above the valley floor.

The Camera Obscura, installed after 1828, allows the viewer a 360° marvellous view around the tower across the Downs and the suspension bridge. A box on top of the building contains a convex lens and sloping mirror. Light is reflected downwards giving an image of the area on to a white circular viewing surface, inside a darkened room. The image is true and not mirrored, and is best seen when the light is bright and sunny.

The gorge runs south to north and cuts through a ridge mainly of limestone, with some sandstone for 1.5 miles. The steep walls of the gorge support some rare fauna and flora, including species unique to the gorge. There are a total of 24 rare plant species and two unique trees. The gorge has a microclimate around 1 degree warmer than the surrounding land. The gorge has Peregrines, large populations of Jackdaw and horseshoe bats, both of which find homes in the caves and bridge buttresses.

In 1754 a £1000 legacy was invested to build a bridge to span the gorge. In 1826 a competition to design the bridge was held and Brunel submitted four different designs. It was begun in 1831 building ceased in 1853 and was not completed until 1864 to a modified version of his original design, due to lack of funding. Even the chains used are second-hand, rescued from the Hungerford Bridge which was being demolished. The Clifton Suspension Bridge spanning the gorge is Brunel's best-known achievement.

Sadly Brunel had died by this time, but the bridge is a lasting testimony to him. The bridge is three foot lower on the Leigh Woods side than the Clifton side to counteract an optical illusion that would make it appear out of true. The bridge spans the 250 foot high beautiful Avon Gorge and links Clifton to Leigh Woods. Over 11,000 vehicles cross it every day. The Visitor Information Centre is at the Leigh Woods end and can provide 45 minute tours.

Only a handful of people have survived the terrible fall from the Clifton Suspension Bridge. The luckiest children were Elsie and Ruby Brown who survived a murder attempt by their father as he could no longer support his family. The howling winds were so violent that up-currents of air somehow caught the falling bodies and cushioned their falls. Both girls fell into the River near a passing pilot boat. They suffered nasty bruises but were back on their feet within days.

Another person, Sarah Ann Henley, was jilted by her boyfriend. She was saved by Victorian women's fashion. This wide skirts and voluminous petticoats l acted like a sort of parachute to break her fall. She drifted in the wind and sailed across to a sticky landing in the deep mud of the riverside. Her rescue from the mud was difficult. She suffered no more than a few light bruises. She later married and lived to the ripe old age of 84.

80 acres of Leigh Woods was given to the National Trust in 1909 by George Wills. The Arboretum was started in the 19th Century. There are some plants and trees that only thrive here; it is a Site of Special Scientific Interest and a National Nature Reserve. In 1949 the forestry commission bought a further 300 acres. The best preserved of the three Iron-Age fort in the gorge is here. There are extensive networks of paths and along the way there are great views across the Gorge at designated vantage points.

In 2005, Ashton Court Estate with 1.7Million visitors was the most popular country park in England. £6 million restoration and development works are in progress with the hope of gaining grade 1 listed status. Ashton Court Estate was acquired by Bristol City Council in 1959. In 1392 Thomas de Lyons was granted a license to enclose his lands and make a park, the foundation of the modern one. It first became a deer park over six hundred years ago.

During the 16th century Ashton Court was bought by John Smyth. It was gradually enlarged, rebuilt, remodelled and reconstructed. It covers 850 acres of woods and grasslands, designed at one time by Humphry Repton who also created Blaise Castle Estate. There are 10 different woodland areas including the Doomsday Oak, which is just one of the many ancient oak trees. The Summerhouse Plantation is full of interesting plants and archaeology.

In 1939 it was requisitioned by the War Office. The last Smyth owner died in 1946.The two main entrances are at Kennel Lodge Road for the mansion and visitor centre of the estate and at Clifton Lodge for the golf course and top of the estate. The visitor centre in the stable block of the mansion provides information on the history of the Estate, a multi-media visitor guide, trail maps and details of activities and events, such as the International Balloon Fiesta.

Clifton Lodge House

There are two 18 hole pitch and putt golf courses, both par 3. The Plateau course is 2663 yards and the Lodge course is 2365 yards. There is a miniature railway on two tracks, one raised and one ground level, each 1/3 of a mile long which is open at selected weekends throughout the year. Special trails include orienteering, mountain biking and horse riding, whose trail is 1.6 miles. Organized fitness sessions are run during the year, including boot camp, wellness and pakrun.

Cabot Tower is built high on a hill on top of Brandon Hill 260 feet above the Harbour behind Park Street. This 105 feet high tower commemorates the 400th anniversary of John Cabot's voyage to Newfoundland in America in 1497. There are fantastic views across the city from the top of the tower. The gardens around the base are a haven for wild life, with butterfly garden, pond, meadow, woodland and heath. There are water features and picnic areas. From ancient times the people of Bristol have been allowed to hang their washing here "on tenter hooks" and to beat carpets.

On the south side of College Green stand the Royal Marriott Hotel, Bristol Cathedral, the facades of four 18th century terraced houses, the Abbey Gatehouse and Bristol Central Library. On the northwest side is the Council House behind a water feature. On the east side the street has a mixture of shops, offices and the Lord Mayor's Chapel. The statues of Queen Victoria and Raja Rammouhun Roy, and a plaque states that the Green still belongs to the Dean and Chapter of the Cathedral.

Within Castle Park are the remnants of Bristol Castle. To control the town, the Normans had only to guard the narrow approach between the rivers. It was demolished in 1650 by Act of Parliament. A few fragments are all that remain of the Castle. Keep, Sallyport, Moat and Walls. After the castle was demolished it became the main shopping area of the city. These streets were severely bombed during WW2.

The buildings that were still standing after the blitz were demolished, and the land was first used as a car park then parkland. The park was completed in 1978, now the paths in Castle Park follow the pre-war roads. Castle Ditch is the moat that once surrounded Bristol Castle and an entrance is hidden away close to Tower Hill Clinic. The moat joined the river Frome to the Avon. There is a gate by Harvey Nicholls that leads from Castle Ditch to ground level.

The sally port was rediscovered in 1991. It was a secure, controlled entryway to the castle, with various means to delay the enemy. It also allowed troops to make sallies, and permit goods to enter, without compromising the defensive strength of fortifications. It opens to a 16-metre long postern tunnel, which ran underneath the south west part of the castle. The tree-lined St Peter's Square, has been home to events including German Christmas markets.

Queen square, named after Queen Anne, is one of the most spacious squares in the kingdom. It was built on marshland. Strict rules had to be followed as to materials and dimensions to be used, for the buildings to harmonize. Work was started in 1708 and completed in 1726. In 1775 seven Africa merchants, one West India merchant and a firm of Virginia tobacco merchants, along with the first overseas American Consulate, established in 1792 lived there.

By the early 19th century many merchants left the Square, where they were away from the bad smells and flooding of the harbour area, to go and live in Clifton. The original Custom House was built in 1711 and destroyed during the Bristol Riots in 1831. The statue in the centre is William III. The Square has been scarred by civil unrest in the 19th Century and by bombs and bulldozers during the 20th but now the modern road bisecting the square has been removed and the Square is back to its elegant best.

The Blaise Castle estate was purchased by the Bristol Corporation in 1926. This 19th century mansion, set in 400 acres of parkland, is home to the social history collection. It includes many household items and everyday objects from centuries past. There are Victorian toilets and baths, kitchen and laundry equipment, model trains, dolls, toys, a Victorian school room and sumptuous period costumes and accessories in the museum.

Blaise Castle estate has been home to an Iron Age hillfort, a Roman temple and a medieval chapel on Castle Hill, you could see for miles in most directions. There are many caves on the Estate, notably Butcher's Cave, whose red tinge to the stones, resembles hanging joints of meat and Robber's cave. Stratford Mill is Grade II listed and was moved to the estate in 1960's. There are five distinct walks which cover all of the different landscapes.

Blaise Estate has a secret garden, first established in the 1800's. In 2013 the Friends of Blaise and Henbury Conservation Society started to restore the garden of almost an acre. Blaise Hamlets is a group of 10 cottages, built in 1809 in differing styles around a green, and were used to house the estate pensioners. They were purchased by the National Trust in 1943. In 1982 Blaise Hamlet was scheduled as an ancient monument, and the preservation of the whole site was assured.

Blaise Hamlets

At the Zoo & botanical gardens there are over 400 exotic and endangered species enclosed in 12 acres of rare beauty and outstanding variety. It is the second oldest zoo in Britain and the fifth oldest zoo in the world. It is governed by 12 Trustees who are elected by the shareholders. Conservation is an important part of the zoos work and has opened a new Wild Place Project on the outskirts of Bristol which has an emphasis on protecting threatened habitats on our doorsteps and around the globe.

In the original zoo there are nine under cover animal houses. There is Monkey Jungle, award winning Seal & Penguin Coasts, award-wining Bug World, Twilight World and the Reptile House. The gardens provide botanical and educational interest. Some feature rare species of plant like 'moth orchids' from the Philippines or the more local Bath asparagus, which are endangered in the wild. Awarded 'Zoo of the Year 2004' by the Good Britain Guide

The Snuff Mills and the surrounding area is a park in the Stapleton area of north Bristol. There are pleasant walks along the steep wooded banks of the River Frome. The park was purchased in 1926 by the Corporation of Bristol as a pleasure walk for citizens of Bristol and restored in the 1980s by the Fishponds Local History Society. The gardens at Snuff Mills have been awarded a Green Flag Award.

Oldbury Court, mentioned in the doomsday book, is further along the river Frome from Snuff mills. By 1485, the estate was in the hands of the Kemys family. By 1715 Robert Winstone had bought the estate and land on both sides of the River. The land passed to Thomas Graeme, the Vassall family and finally to Bristol Corporation. A fire in 1948 severely damaged the coach house and stables. By 1949 the house had also been demolished.

Sparke Evans Park is situated on the river Avon, the land was donated by P.F. Sparke and Jonathan Evans, local tannery owners, in 1902. It was built when the Marsh was a residential area, but it has become almost totally industrial. There is a bridge linking the park and from the residents of Arno's Vale across the river. A shelter (pictured) dating from 1925 can be seen on the far west of the park featuring wrought-iron pillars, with ornate and decorative brackets.

Victoria Park has tennis, bowling and three measured miles. In the park there is a water maze, copied from a roof-boss in St. Mary Redcliffe Church. It was built by Avon County Conservation and Environmental Scheme and opened in l984. The maze marks the spot where the 12th century Redcliffe Pipe, which carried fresh water from Knowle to Redcliffe Church, and the 20th century Southern Foul Water Interceptor Tunnel, carrying sewage to Avonmouth to be treated, meet.

The 70 acres Eastville park was purchased from Ashton Court estate in 1889 by Bristol Corporation. It was constructed as part of a social scheme instigated by MP Ernest Bevin. There was once a swimming pool but it was war damaged. The bowling greens with the Nissan shelter clubhouse, are still in use. It is a community footballing venue. The Park holds community events reflecting the multicultural and diverse population of the areas.

Berkeley Square was laid out around 1790 in Georgian style, with a central grass area behind railings. At No 23 Berkeley Square, John McAdam lived. The Bristol Civic Society purchased the remains of Bristol's replica High Cross in 1950 and re-erected the truncated remains in the garden of the square. The buildings damaged during the Blitz were rebuilt to maintain the same facade.

Arno's Court has an Arch. The arch used to stand in front of the building, but was moved in 1912 about 100 metres away. Much of the freestone carving and dressings are reputed to have come from the city's demolished medieval gateways, and St Werburghs Church. The original statues were those from Newgate and Lawfords' Gate when they were demolished. It has been designated by English Heritage as a grade I listed building. In 1850 Arno's Court became a Roman Catholic convent and girl's reformatory school. Girls from as far as Manchester were sent there for such heinous crimes as stealing a reel of cotton. The convent survived until 1948, and in 1960 the house began a new lease of life as a hotel and nightclub.

Troopers Hill was purchased by Bristol City Council in 1956 for use as a public open space. The hill was largely left to take care of itself and seems to have remained largely unchanged until the early 1990s. Troopers Hill was declared as a Local Nature Reserve in 1995 in recognition of the wide range of wildlife present on the hill and its importance as a unique habitat in the Bristol area due to the presence of acidic soils.

109

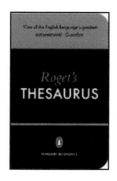

Dowry Square probably has the strangest associations having the affections of literary types, drinkers, dentists and drug addicts. Here, early in 1812, the economic migrant Jacob Schweppe opened his fizz factory. Dr Thomas Beddoes also ran his clinic, attempting to cure consumption by introducing cows into the patients' bedrooms. He and his assistant Humphrey Davy did much for the happiness of nations by producing nitrous oxide, popular as a recreational drug. Another assistant, Peter Roget, compiled the Thesaurus. Beddoes' son, Thomas Lovell, was one of Bristol's greatest poets.

Stoke Park is an 18th Century landscape, has grade II* aspects, the balustraded terrace, the Orangery, the remains of the Obelisk, and the Broomhill Gate. The open space of 270 acres is found alongside the M32 motorway and was acquired by Bristol City Council in spring 2011. Within Stoke Park are two small lakes, the largest of which is Duchess Pond, the Dower House, built in 1553, the Beaufort Memorial, the cold bath and a partially derelict stone tunnel with entrance arches

Purdown is a ridge of land where prehistoric settlements and bronze age fragments have been found. Where the name Purdown comes from no one is sure. It is a continuation of the Stoke Park estate, but there is no boundary fence between the two. The BT Tower is used for point-to-point microwave links and was built in 1970. It is visible from much of the city. It is one of twelve reinforced concrete towers owned by BT in the UK. It is also used for radio broadcasting to the Bristol area.

During WW2 the ridge housed an anti-aircraft site. It was thought that an immense supergun, 'Purdown Percy' was housed there but in fact emplacement was armed with four high-velocity cannon that went off simultaneously. The ruined camp, gun bases and magazines were scheduled as an Ancient Monument in the 1980s. Sir John's Lane is the remains of a mediaeval road, known locally as stony lane, which went from Stoke Gifford, past Stoke Lodge, to the City Centre.

Purdown Ridge

Hanham Mills is halfway along the old roman road linking Bristol and Bath and an ancient ferry crossed here. The weir powered several mills, including a grist Mill. The lock opened in 1727, thus improving the passage of coal and quarry stone to Bath. In 1690 water was pumped from the river to the duck pond and then through hollow elm logs to a reservoir in Lawrence Hill. For an annual cost residents could buy "fresh" river water rather than well water.

The open space of Whitchurch airport is now known as Hengrove Park. At the west end of the park there is an unusual bowl-shaped area rich in wildlife and grasses. The southern edge of the park has been given over to Hengrove Park Leisure Centre, The South Bristol Community Hospital, The South Bristol Skills Academy and The Bottle Yard Studios, which is the largest dedicated film and TV studio facility in the West of England.

In 1882 Adolf Leipner laid out a botanic garden on waste ground near to Royal Fort House in Clifton. The garden moved to Tyndall Avenue then Bracken Hill and finally the Holmes (pictured). It cultivates over 4,500 plants within its five-acre site that are not found in the Bristol area. The glasshouses hold the Amazon rainforest, the Highveld in South Africa, the cloud forests and a magical world of tropical food and medicinal plants.

Netham Park is next to the Feeder canal and the path along its edge is the Avon Valley Cycleway and pedestrian route into the city centre. There are a number of football pitches, a cricket pitch, and an area for other sports such as lacrosse a floodlit multi-use games area, a bowling green, changing rooms and clubhouse, a pavilion, public toilets, a community room and kiosk, and staff offices. The site has meadow and woodland areas. It is a Nature Conservation site.

Greville Smyth Park was originally part of Ashton Court Estate, and is now a community park, well known for its trees, views, play area and community-led activity programme. A specimen Indian Bean Tree grows below the tennis courts on the eastern edge of the park. There are tennis courts football pitches, and bowling green. Friends of Greville Smyth work on event and developmental work. It has been awarded Green Flag status since 2012.

Canford Park was opened as a municipal park 1874. The park was taken over by the corporation in 1904. It has five gated entrances. The park is flat with many paths. There is a shrubbery, sunken garden with a lily-pond, rose beds, several mature trees and two Indian bean trees. There is a Grade II listed drinking fountain, which dates from 1897, bowling green and pavilion, two tennis courts, two football pitches and café kiosk

Horfield Common is an open space with a long history of grazing with rights to one horse, two cows or three yearlings. Poplar Cottage was demolished in 1926 and was rebuilt and named Ardagh (pictured). Ardagh bowling green and tennis courts has been built in its grounds. The South Gloucestershire Regiment was in Horfield from 1845. The Territorial Army remains. In 1908 Horfield Common was acquired by the Council. The leisure centre has a 25 m swimming pool.

St Georges Park was created on Fire Engine Farm in 1894. It became the responsibility of the city council in 1897. It has an avenue of plane trees and a lake. Today there is a dog-free playground, large wheels skate park, basketball hoops, tennis courts and a bowling green. Only the original Victorian entrance gates remain from the structures built for the park during the 19th century; the bandstand has long disappeared. Various small festivals are held during the year.

St. Andrews Park is a classic Victorian neighbourhood park. It was officially opened in 1895. There is a tea room, paddling pool, enclosed dog-free children's play area and bowling green. There are mature trees and ornamental trees and shrubs. A Wellington bomber crashed in WW2 in 1941 when three of the six-man crew died in the accident. In 2009 a memorial stone was erected and in 2011 there was a short 70 year anniversary service.

Portland Square is a Grade I listed square. In the early 18th century it was one of Bristol's first suburbs, with its central focus of St. Paul's Church. It is laid out around central gardens. The gates and railings are a grade II listed. In the 19th century there was boot & shoe manufacture, ink and cardboard box making. A raid in 1940 killed 40 people and destroyed the North of the Square and the area stayed as a ruin for many years. It was designated as a Conservation Area in 1974. The Circomedia centre for circus and theatre training opened in 2004, in St Pauls church.

Brunswick Square has red brick town houses and was started in 1771. The communal garden dates from 1788. Brunswick Chapel has iconic columns, a rendered front and was built in 1834. Most of the houses in the square are grade II listed. The Unitarian Meeting House was the Surrey Lodge to the burial ground. The square was acquired by the Council in 1952, and the grass was restored and the rose beds planted.

The national cycle network started in Bristol. Cycle Bristol Action Group, shortened to Cyclebag was formed in 1977. Permission was granted to convert part of a rail route from Bath to Bitton. Between 1979 and 1986 the railway line was converted into the Railway Path. The path follows the course of the old Midland Railway which closed for passenger traffic at the end of the 1960s. The action group was reformed as Sustrans (sustainable transport).

Another section of Path is part of the former Avon and Gloucestershire Railway which was built to carry coal from Kingswood's Coalpit Heath collieries near Yate down to the River Avon. Today the 3 metre wide Railway Path begins just off the Midland Road and runs through to the centre of Bath, via Mangotsfield, Warmley and Saltford. The path contains features of the railway past, especially the stations at Bitton and Warmley, a tunnel and the bridges carrying overhead roads.

There are a variety of pubs near the old stations on route to take refreshments, especially in the suburbs. The walkway into central Bristol follows the course of the river Avon from Midland road. Cyclists can follow a different route. It has proved to be a source of inspiration to many artists and craftspeople that have created over a dozen pieces of public art along the route. The rural appearance makes it popular as there are views across the city and its suburbs.

Another cycle path goes between Queen Square, Bristol and Portishead, travelling over the grade 2 listed old harbour road rail bridge, along the River Avon and through the Gorge. The path passes under the Clifton Suspension Bridge, through Leigh Woods, Ham Green and Pill, before finishing in Portishead. It is 11.5 miles long and is a mix of traffic-free routes, purpose-built cycleways and quiet roads.

22 Famous Bristolians.

William Penn was the son of Admiral Sir William Penn who helped restore Charles II to the throne. The King owed Penn and traded 47,000 acres of American land for cash. William and his Quaker community sailed over to America. On founding Pennsylvania in 1682 he declared, 'Let every house be placed in the middle of its plot so there may be ground on each side for gardens or orchards or fields.' A few years later came the edict, 'Every owner of a house should plant one or more trees before the door that the town may be well shaded from the violence of the sun.' The garden city had arrived thanks to a Bristolian. In 1696 Penn's son, also named William, married Hannah Callowhill in the meeting house at Quakers Friars, Bristol.

Robert Southey was a Romantic poet and Poet Laureate. He was born at No. 9 Wine Street in 1774. Since the WW2 bombing the house no longer exists, but there is a plaque on the post-war office building. There is a bust of Southey in the cathedral. Thomas Chatterton was the boy-poet, but never gained much fame outside Bristol. He was born near St Mary Redcliffe, in 1752. He went to London to find fame and fortune, but committed suicide there at the age of 17 when he found his talents unrecognised.

Bristol was a driving force for the romantic poets with William Wordsworth, Robert Southey, Charles Lamb and Samuel Taylor Coleridge all coming to the city to work. Joseph Cottle produced the first poems of these poets. Cottle was held in high esteem as a publisher and bookseller, he also wrote many poems. He went into partnership with Nathaniel Biggs to form the publishers Biggs and Cottle.

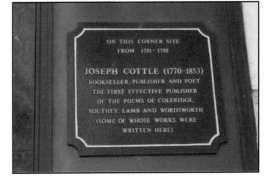

Sir Allen Lane was born in 1902 and became founder of Penguin Books in 1935. Lane decided that good quality contemporary fiction should be made available at an attractive price and sold not just in traditional bookshops, but also in railway stations, tobacconists and chain stores. The first Penguin paperbacks included works by Ernest Hemingway, André Maurois and Agatha Christie. They were colour coded, orange for fiction, blue for biography, green for crime and cost just sixpence. Years later Penguin is still one of the most recognizable brands in the world.

Richard Savage claimed to be the illegitimate son of the Countess of Macclesfield, and the 4th Earl of Rivers. He was known best as a satirist. In 1727 he was arrested for the murder of James Sinclair but escaped the death penalty. He was imprisoned for debt in Bristol. Savage died in prison in 1743. Francis Greenway was born in Mangotsfield and was an architect His only remaining building in Bristol is the Clifton Hotel and Assembly Rooms. For the crime of forgery he was sentenced to death; this sentence was later commuted to 14 years transportation.

Bristol can also boast a variety of artists. Edward Hodges Baily who was born in 1788. He became a pupil of Flaxman and is best known for the 16 ft high figure of Nelson on the column in Trafalgar Square, London. He was also employed by George IV to make sculptures for both Buckingham Palace and Admiralty Arch. The frieze over the entrance to the Freemasons' Hall in Park Street is an example of his work. Samuel Jackson, noted water-colour painter of the Bristol School, lived in several places in Bristol, including Freeland Place. Jackson's only well-known oil, View of Avon at Hotwells painted about 1836, actually shows Freeland Place in the background.

Banksy is an urban street artist whose work has sprung up throughout Bristol and around the world. He took over the city art museum in the 2010 to showcase his distinct style. Some of Banksy's works are worth more than the building or structure they are sprayed on. Bristol has become famous for street art and The See No Evil exhibition has transformed the Nelson Street buildings into an open air urban art centre, with buildings covered with artwork.

Mary Carpenter, whose name is well-known in the field of social reform, was born in Exeter in 1807. Her father was Minister of the Unitarian Chapel in Lewins Mead (pictured), Bristol from 1780 to 1840. In the mid-19th century the Bristol streets were full of homeless and destitute children. Her book Juvenile Delinquency was instrumental in the passing of the Juvenile Offenders' Act of 1854 and in that year she opened a reform school for girls in the Red Lodge.

116

Hannah More was born in Fishponds in 1745. Hannah became a teacher and was involved with the Theatre Royal. Her tragedy, Percy, was staged at the Covent Garden Theatre. Her poem, Slavery, coincided with the first parliamentary debate on the slave trade. In 1789, she founded her first Sunday school at Cheddar (pictured). In retirement, she wrote best-selling works of Evangelical piety, and was active in the anti-slavery movement. She was a most successful writers and influential woman.

Agnes Beddoe moved to Bristol in 1858 and was an active feminist, and suffragette. She became a Poor Law Guardian and was a member of the Women's Liberal Association, the Industrial School Committee, and a governor of Red Maids' School, acted as a local examiner for the University of Edinburgh and formed the Bristol Emigration Society to help women and pauper children find homes in the colonies. She established a Home for Working Girls, in 1889 for women trying to lead honest, respectable lives, and to assist them in lifting themselves out of poverty and into respectability.

Miss Susanna Winkworth was a philanthropist, author and translator. She worked among the poor and rented several houses in the poorest part of the town, and letting them out in tenements. She was the first in Bristol to make efforts for the better housing of the poor and in 1874 she formed the company which built Jacob's Wells industrial dwellings, managing them herself till the time of her death. She took a great interest in the education of women, and in 1878 succeeded her sister Catherine as governor of the Red Maids' school.

George Müller cared for 10,024 orphans in his life. He established 117 schools. In 1836 he opened his home at 6 Wilson Street, Bristol and housed thirty girls. Three more houses bringing the total of children cared for to 130. In 1849 Ashley Down opened to house 300 children. By 1870, there was room for 2,050 children accommodated in five homes. In 1958 the children moved out and it became the Bristol College of Science and Technology, later the City of Bristol College, Brunel Campus.

Norah Fry was born and educated in Clifton in 1871. She was an advocate for better services for people with learning disabilities. She was very concerned about the lack of proper schools for disabled children and the shortage of housing for people with learning disabilities. For over fifty years she was a member of the council of Bristol University and had a very close relationship with university staff. Norah Fry some money to set up the Department of Mental Health.

Elizabeth Blackwell was born in Queens Square Bristol in 1821. The family emigrated to the USA in 1832. Elizabeth enrolled in a medical school, but lost the sight of one eye which prevented further progress as a surgeon, but she went to work at St Bartholomew's in London. In the USA in 1851 she met hostility when opening the New York Infirmary for Women and Children with all female medical staff. She came back to England and became the first woman to be enrolled on the British Medical register. She campaigned for the admission of women and reforms in the medical profession, visiting Bristol frequently.

Eliza Walker Dunbar was one of the seven women to receive a medical degree from the University of Zurich. In 1873 she was appointed house surgeon at the Hospital for Sick Children but most doctors walked out. Eliza resigned and opened the Read Dispensary for Women and Children. She was allowed to practice medicine in 1877. In 1895 she started the Bristol Private Hospital for Women and Children and worked there until her death in 1925.

Emma Saunders worked with girls in a Bristol industrial home, and with children in a "Ragged School". Ragged schools were charitable organisations to give free education to destitute children in the 19th-century, with an emphasis on reading, writing, arithmetic, and bible studies. She founded the Bristol and West of England Railwaymen's Institute, which contained leisure facilities as well as a room for engineering classes and religious meetings. Her temperance movement tried to prevent young railway staff succumbing to the temptations of the demon drink by giving out Christian literature and flowers. A plaque is at the main entrance to Bristol Temple Meads railway station.

Art Satherley was born in 1889 and raised in Bedminster, Bristol. In 1913 he left for America and became involved in the new and developing recording industry. He became head of A&R for the CBS record label until his retirement in 1952. In 1968 the Academy of Country Music awarded their first "Pioneer Award" to Art and in 1971 he was inducted into the Country Music Hall of Fame for his work as a record pioneer, the only Englishman to be awarded this honour. Satherley died in Los Angeles in 1986.

Bristol singer Elsie Griffin started work at Fry's Chocolates, Keynsham and sang with the 'Fry's Angels'. She also took sewing jobs to fund singing lessons. In 1914, Elsie won a singing scholarship at the Bristol Eisteddfod. She recorded 'Danny Boy' and 'Roses of Picardy', and entertained First World War troops. After the war, she sang for the D'Oyly Carte and Carl Rosa opera companies. Her version of 'Poor Wandering One' was named Best British Gramophone Solo in 1929 and she performed around the world until the late 1950s.

Famous actors include Cary Grant, born Archibald Alec Leach in Hughenden Road, Horfield. His mother was placed in an institution. He worked doing odd jobs at the Hippodrome and Empire and in 1920 he went to the USA with a troupe of acrobats and vaudeville. His Hollywood career began in the 1930s when he signed for Paramount, where he was told to change his name. He then moved to Columbia Pictures and starred in romantic comedies and four Hitchcock films. He often revisited Bristol to see his mother. A statue of him can be found in Millennium Square. He married five times and died at the age of 82. In 1970 he was awarded a Special Lifetime Achievement Academy Award.

Bob Hope's home in toddler days was at 326 Whitehall Road, Bristol. He had a scar as a permanent reminder of Bristol. He tried to protect his dog whilst some boys were ill-treating it. One of them threw a stone and it hit him on the temple. He emigrated to America in 1908, and became an entertainer, film actor and comedian. He received more than 2,000 awards including an honorary knighthood from the Queen in 1998. He lived until he was 100.

Kingswood born television presenter Johnny Ball is one of the 50 icons included in the Bristol Zoo Gardens Walk of Fame. He was one of the hosts of infant education programme Play School at the start of BBC2 in 1964. He became a regular fixture on children's television in the late 1970s and the 1980s. His forte was science and mathematics. He wrote and presented 23 television series. Think of a Number and Think Again TV shows were made here.

Russ Conway was born in Southville in 1925. He became a pianist for top artists like Dennis Lotis, Gracie Fields and Joan Regan. In 1957 he signed with EMI, and recorded a medley of old sing-along tunes in a honky-tonk style (Party Pops), which was a hit at Christmas that year. He started to appear on TV shows like the Billy Cotton Band Show. Five of his own compositions made the Top 10 with two going to No 1. Side Saddle stayed at the top spot for four weeks, making Russ the top-selling UK artist in 1959.

Bristol photographer William Friese-Greene lived in College Street and patented schemes ranging from air-ship bombs and stereo colour film to X-ray apparatus. In 1889 he took out Patent No. 10131 for a projector which took and showed moving pictures by using opaque film with slotted holes which could be run through a camera to record scenes in close sequence. He sent Edison precise details of the mechanism involved because he hoped for a joint project to ally Edison's phonograph with the Friese-Greene camera but Edison never replied. He went to the U.S. courts to prove he had patented his invention before Edison. He won; therefore Friese-Greene was the Father of the Cinema.

Famous Bristol scientists and industrialists include Humphrey Davy who resided in Dowry Square, Hotwells. Davy investigated nitrous oxide, also known as laughing gas, using equipment designed by James Watt. He went to the Royal Institution in London and became professor of chemistry. He also invented the Davy lamp used by coal miners as a replacement for the candles used previously. In 1810 it used charcoal elements and was powered by batteries enclosed in a vacuum. A variety of improvements followed until an electric current was used for the regulation of the carbons.

Paul Adrien Maurice Dirac was born in Bishopston in 1902 and attended Bishop Primary school. He attended Bristol University in 1918, and he graduated with first-class honours in both electrical engineering and mathematics. His work led to the joint award of a Nobel Prize for Quantum Mechanics in 1933. He published the Principles of Quantum Mechanics and other scientific papers. He predicted the existence of antiparticles, which are now called positrons. When he died in Florida in 1984, Stephen Hawking commented "Paul Dirac has done more than anyone this century, with the exception of Einstein, to advance physics and change our picture of the universe."

John James was born in Bedminster in 1906 his legacy lives on in the John James Bristol Foundation established in 1983. He died in 1996. The main areas of focus are education, health and the elderly. His first gift of £12,000 in 1963 met the cost of a Bristol Old Folks' Festival. This Festival proved to be a great success and was able to grow. Outings were added and all the expenses were paid for. The final Festival week was held in 1996. However, grants continue to be made to charitable organisations for the benefit of Bristol residents.

Thomas' Goldney was a rich merchant who sent his ships to some of the world's most exotic places. Their secondary orders were to collect shells, sparkling stones, coral and other bright and shiny pieces for the grotto he began to build in 1737. Thomas Goldney's grotto in Clifton took nearly 30 years to complete and is a place of glints, lights and sparkles and one of the best follies in the world. His home and garden now belong to Bristol University and the garden and fabulous cave are occasionally open to the public. .

Ernest Bevin moved to Bristol from Winsford and formed a branch of the Dockers' Union in 1910. In 1921 Bevin set up the Transport and General Workers' Union and became the first Secretary to the organisation. During the Second World War he became a member of Churchill's Cabinet and was made Minister of Labour and National Service. He introduced a scheme for young conscripts to work in the coal mines rather than join the armed forces, the workers being known colloquially as Bevin Boys. Between 1945 -1951 he was Foreign Secretary.

Mural on Stapleton Road Station

Ben Tillett, born Easton, Bristol in 1860 began the first unions for unskilled workers. He was the leader of the Great London Dock Strike of 1889 and Alderman of London County Council. In 1928 he became chair of the Trades Union Congress. A founder of the Independent Labour Party in 1893 and was Labour MP for Salford, 1917-24 & 1929-31. He was co-founder of the national newspaper "The Daily Herald" to compete with the newspapers that supported the Liberals and Conservatives.

William Gilbert Grace, the famous cricketer known as WG, was born in Downend in 1848. Between 1865 and 1908 he captained Gloucestershire for 28 of those years and also played for England during most of that time. He scored 126 centuries and had a bowling record of 2809 wickets throughout his career. He qualified and practiced as a doctor. He also was the first president of the English Bowling Association (lawn bowls). He lived in Easton and Clifton. A pub in Clifton and one near the county ground are named after him.

J W Arrowsmith came to Bristol in the 1850's. He was head of one of Bristol's largest printing firms. The best known publication was Three Men in a Boat by Jerome K. Jerome in 1889. JW won the Albert Jewel for rifle shooting. He was President of Bristol Rugby FC, joint secretary of the Industrial and Fine Art Exhibition and helped create Bristol University. JW was Hon. Secretary and Treasurer of the Mary Carpenter Memorial Boys Home, Chairman of Bristol Liberal Club and Secretary of the campaign to erect Cabot Tower. In 1894, he founded Arrow bowling club, and became a Justice of the Peace. In 1902 the West of England and South Wales Coronation Bowling League was formed with JW as President. The clubs were Arrow, Pontypool, MacKintosh and Victoria.

Robin Cousins from Sea Mills is the 1980 Olympic champion figure skater and European champion, a three-time World medallist and four-time British national champion. His back flip entered the Guinness Book of Records. In 1980 was the BBC Sports Personality of the Year and received the MBE. He later starred in and produced ice shows; appeared in theatre productions and was inducted into the World Figure Skating Hall of Fame. In 2005 was head judge on ITV's Dancing on Ice.

Nipper was a mongrel with a touch of bull terrier and a century later he's still celebrated for his role as that loyal pooch listening to His Master's Voice. The Bristol-born dog was bought as a pup in 1884 by flamboyant Bristol theatrical artist Mark Barraud and the two became inseparable. Mark Barraud brother, Francis, painted the picture of Nipper listening to the gramophone in 1899 and so HMV was coined.

Other famous Bristolians include Canon Hardwicke Drummond Rawnsley who was born in 1851. He was a poet, writer of hymns and conservationist who co-founded The National Trust in 1895. Anna Maria who, during the 1889 Bristol cotton workers' strikes, set up a soup kitchen for the strikers. Jessie Stephen was born in 1893. She was a trade unionist and councillor who in 1952 became the first woman president of the trade's council.

23 Retail Therapy

Shopping in Bristol offers plenty of choice. In the town is Broadmead, which incorporates Cabot Circus and the Mall Galleries, and has all the familiar high street names and specialist independent stores. In the old city is St Nicholas Market, and just outside, Christmas Steps. There are the elegant shops of Bristol's West End, Whiteladies Road and Clifton Village. Where there are cafes and restaurants, bookshops, antiques, jewellery and designer clothes.

In 1740 permission was granted to build a street 40 feet wide up to the parklands surrounding Royal Fort. Park Street, known as the West End, rises steeply from College Green. The Georgian townhouses were gradually converted into shops during Victorian times. Park Street was shortlisted for the Great British High Street of the Year Award 2014 and boasts a wide selection of independent stores.

Established in 1743 for the sale of fruit and vegetables, St Nicholas market is the oldest market in Bristol. Over 50 stalls provide a wide variety of goods and food items. Divided into three sections, The Glass Arcade with its new roof, is nestled between the quieter "Covered Market" and the "Indoor Exchange", It is home to the largest collection of independent retailers in Bristol and is commonly known as St Nicks.

Entrances can be found in Corn Street, High Street and St Nicholas Street. The Exchange was built in 1741-43 and a corn market was held there. By 1869 a roof was added to the central hall. The Exchange was designated as a Grade I listed building. The market floor contains everything from old photographic print stands or clothes and jewellery stalls. The Glass Arcade has food outlets, florists and textiles sellers. The Covered Market contains many bookshops.

In the nearby streets you will find regular street markets, including the nails market, antiques, arts and crafts every Friday and Saturday, Saturday fresh food market, a Farmers Market every Wednesday, and the Slow Food Market takes place on the first Sunday of each month. Also there are other special events throughout the year such as Italian AutoMoto Festival and 'make Sunday special' where the whole of Corn Street is closed to traffic.

In the 15th century Broadmead was a meadow from which it derived its name. It developed around a 13th century Dominican friary and was a mixture of 16th to 19th century housing, shops, chapels and small workshops. By 1930, Broadmead shopping area had fallen behind Wine Street and Castle Street. Both areas were devastated by WW2 bombs. After the war Broadmead was re-developed, and in recent years, two undercover shopping Malls were built, the Galleries and Cabot Circus.

On the outskirts of Bristol, The Mall at Cribbs Causeway is a shopping complex with over 135 stores and over 17 cafes and restaurants, all under one roof. It is classed as a regional shopping centre and has two large department stores, Marks & Spencer and John Lewis, along with all the normal high street stores. It is situated near junction 17 of the M5 and was built on 5 farms of greenbelt land. It was opened in 1998 and there is parking for 7000 cars. The Venue and other large shops are in adjacent areas.

24 The Future

Creativity, innovation and sustainability are factors that Bristol has always prided itself on. Bristol has been included in Rockefeller Foundation's 100 Resilient Cities. It is a programme intended to help cities "become more resilient to the physical, social, and economic challenges that are a growing part of the 21st century". Its aim is to help "individuals, communities, institutions, businesses, and systems within a city to survive, adapt, and grow no matter what kinds of chronic stresses and acute shocks they experience".

A set of businessmen have produced a blueprint for the year 2050. One suggestion extends the Floating Harbour by putting a barrage in the Avon Gorge, close to the Clifton Suspension Bridge. This could lead to the reshaping of the city centre and the Cumberland basin area of the city, creating a water park. Another is to build an opera house and velodrome, in addition to the indoor arena, that is about to be built. Finally, to create a new transport hub, that will serve the southern half of the city.

Bristol has a long involvement in speed and The Bloodhound Project is no exception. It is first and foremost an education project, but it is hoping to exceed 1000mph to achieve a land speed record. The project was based in building by the harbourside. The Bloodhound technical centre is in Avonmouth. The bloodhound will have three power units, a Eurojet EJ200 jet engine, a Nammo hybrid rocket and an auxiliary Jaguar V-8 engine. The attempt is due to take place in 2016.

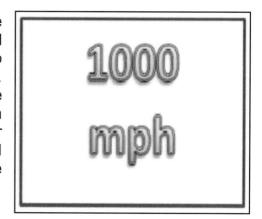

ABOUT THE AUTHOR

Ever since being told that Muller Road was the longest residential road without a pub, and that the first lady doctor in the world was born in Bristol, Teresa became interested in learning all she could about the city where she was born.

Teresa spent her working career as a Teacher of Mathematics and P.E. She still lives in Bristol, England with her Civil Partner.

Teresa enjoys cruising holidays, playing bowls and darts as well as watching her local football team Bristol Rovers.

She hopes you find this tome full of interesting facts and pictures.

ACKNOWLEDGMENTS

Thanks to everyone who provided me with all the snippets of information I have been given over the years, without which this book would never have been written.

Thank you Gill for your support and critical eye.

Thanks to Steve for his editorial skills and suggestions.

Made in the USA
Charleston, SC
17 November 2016